The white kangeroo : a tale of colonial life founded on fact

E Davenport Cleland

Nabu Public Domain Reprints:

You are holding a reproduction of an original work published before 1923 that is in the public domain in the United States of America, and possibly other countries. You may freely copy and distribute this work as no entity (individual or corporate) has a copyright on the body of the work. This book may contain prior copyright references, and library stamps (as most of these works were scanned from library copies). These have been scanned and retained as part of the historical artifact.

This book may have occasional imperfections such as missing or blurred pages, poor pictures, errant marks, etc. that were either part of the original artifact, or were introduced by the scanning process. We believe this work is culturally important, and despite the imperfections, have elected to bring it back into print as part of our continuing commitment to the preservation of printed works worldwide. We appreciate your understanding of the imperfections in the preservation process, and hope you enjoy this valuable book.

THE WHITE KANGAROO.

"Slowly making their way through a belt of scrub, they were suddenly startled by the appearance of two natives."—*See Page* 107.

Frontispiece.

THE WHITE KANGAROO.

A Tale of Colonial Life.

FOUNDED ON FACT

BY

E. DAVENPORT CLELAND.

Illustrated.

LONDON:
WELLS GARDNER, DARTON, & CO.,
2 PATERNOSTER BUILDINGS, E.C.

1890

CONTENTS.

CHAP.		PAGE
I.	HOMEWARD BOUND	1
II	AT HOME	5
III	WILLAROO	10
IV.	'POSSUMS	21
V.	"PEPPER"	32
VI.	FRIENDLY BLACKS	37
VII.	RUMOURS OF WILD BLACKS	43
VIII.	SMITH'S TWO FRIENDS	48
IX.	"THE SHAKING" MALLEE TREE	54
X.	SPORT AT NIGHT	63
XI	SUNDAY AT WILLAROO	71
XII.	OFF TO THE OUT-STATION	77
XIII.	THEIR FIRST KANGAROO	84
XIV.	LOST	90
XV.	CAPTURED BY BLACKS	102
XVI.	THE BLACK ENCAMPMENT	112
XVII	LIFE WITH THE BLACKS	121
XVIII.	THE NATIVES PREPARE FOR A JOURNEY	131
XIX.	PLANS OF ESCAPE	136
XX.	A PITCH DARK NIGHT	142
XXI	A SEARCH PARTY	147
XXII.	TRACKING	154
XXIII.	THE MIRAGE	163
XXIV.	FOUND	171
XXV.	THE WHITE KANGAROO	175

THE WHITE KANGAROO.

CHAPTER I.

HOMEWARD BOUND

THE stage-coach which carried Her Majesty's mails through a part of her dominions in South Australia was travelling northwards through the heat and dust of a December day. Mile after mile had it bumped over the rough roads, swinging from side to side. Five horses drew it along, two in the pole and three abreast in the lead; strong, active animals, well adapted to draw the heavy load.

Upon the box beside the driver sat two boys, their hats pressed tightly down, and their heads bent to meet the wind. They were fresh from school, and were bound for a sheep-station in the north, where they were going to pass their holidays. The elder of the two, Ralph Everdale, was a lad of fourteen, and the other, his cousin, Ernest Everdale, a year younger. They had taken their seats upon the box on the afternoon of the previous day, and had kept them ever since, except when a change of horses gave them time to stretch their legs. All through the night had they travelled, and now the sun was again near its setting. At last it disappeared beneath the horizon, looking like a globe of fire; quickly the light faded away, and the night came. It was pleasant to get rid of the sun for a time, and to make matters pleasanter the wind decreased in force. Very soon the moon rose and lit up the great treeless plain across which the travellers were moving; and as Ralph looked at it he exclaimed, "What a glorious moon for 'possum shooting!"

"Yes, isn't it!" answered Ernest. "Are there as many about the station as last year?"

"Just about, though the blacks killed a number in the winter. You remember that big gum-tree that stands near the wool-shed?"

"Yes, of course! Why, didn't I very nearly break my neck tumbling off it?"

"So you did. Well, not long after that we got five 'possums and a wild cat out of it."

"That was a piece of luck! I hope we shall have the same these holidays."

"I know a capital place some distance up the creek where wallabies are as plentiful as currants in a cake."

"What sort of cake do you mean? If there are not more wallabies than there were currants in the cake they gave us at the eating-house, it won't be worth while to go out shooting."

"That's hard on the cake, Ernest. But from the way you ate it you thought it fairly good."

"You ate your share anyhow, not to speak of the lump you put in your pocket!"

"Well, I had quite forgotten that," and as he spoke Ralph drew forth a large lump of heavy cake. "Have a piece, Ernest?"

"Yes, I don't mind; but you can keep that pen-nib and that bit of slate-pencil attached to it." As Ernest spoke he picked those articles from the lump he held. "Well," he said, as he took the last bite, "it wasn't bad; but I'll tell you one thing that I would rather have just now than all the cake in the world."

"It must be something very good then, because if a fellow had all the cake in the world he could exchange it for lots of things, such as guns, and tops, and cricketing things!"

"I would like a jolly big tub full of ice-cold water, or a plunge in the baths in Adelaide."

"It will take a lot of water to get rid of all this dust, won't it?"

"It will so, and I suppose you are just as short of water at the station as ever?"

"I expect so; but we *must* have a bath. If we don't use too much soap, it will do for the dogs to drink afterwards, so it won't be wasted."

"Well, I shall be glad when this journey comes to an end, for I am pretty tired of it."

"Just wait till we get over this rise in front of us, and we ought to see the wool-shed, and then it is only a mile to the house. Yes, there it is! See, Ernest! And look, under the shadow of the hill beyond you can see the house! Do you hear that dog barking? That is old Rover, I am sure!"

The sight of his home, not seen for twelve months, aroused such enthusiasm in Ralph, that at the top of his voice he sang "Home, sweet Home." The melody was infectious. Every one of the passengers joined in, and in the midst of the song the coach drove up to the station.*

---

* Station—the term applied in the colonies to the homesteads of the sheep-farmers or squatters.

CHAPTER II.

AT HOME.

The coach had dropped the boys about twenty yards from the house. Mr. Everdale was there to meet them with one or two of the men.

"Well, boys, I *am* glad to see you!" Mr. Everdale exclaimed, as he shook them by the hand. "This is a quiet, sleepy place, when there is no one about but old people such as Brown and Munroe here and myself! So you two must make as much noise as ever you can, and get into all the scrapes possible to enliven us. Do you think you can manage to do that, boys, if you try very hard?"

"We'll do our best, father!" said Ralph, laughing, and thinking how different his father was from those strict masters at school.

"Don't you think you'll be tired of us, uncle, before the week ends?" asked Ernest, looking up from a collie dog he was making friends with.

"Not a bit of it, my boy! not a bit of it! The only limit I shall put upon your amusements will be that they hurt no one, and that you have some consideration for others. But, come, let us go to the house. Run on ahead, boys. See, there is your mother, Ralph, waiting for you, and wondering why you are standing here talking so long."

By this time the boys had raced across to the house, and Mrs. Everdale, heedless alike of their dust-laden faces or the damage she was doing to the brims of their hats, put her arms round first her son and then her nephew, and kissed them lovingly. What a happy meeting that was! Ralph had been away during the whole year, and Ernest had not been up at the station for two years. He had spent his last summer holidays elsewhere. When they entered the room they were critically examined by both Mr. and Mrs. Everdale to see how much they had grown and altered. And then came the all-important subject of supper. Notwithstanding the amount of dust they had swallowed, both boys were as hungry as all healthy boys should be. But first came the question of the bath, and, much to their delight, they found they might use as much water as they wished. A new well had been sunk close to the house, and a good supply of fresh water had been struck. It was at a great depth though, and had to be raised by horse-power into large tanks. In a few minutes Ralph and Ernest were splashing about in the bath-room, much after the manner of a couple of hippopotami at play, their merry voices waking up the echoes of the old house, startling an antiquated family of opossums that lived under the roof, and causing the maid-servants to feel that the monotony of their lives was to be pleasantly broken into for some weeks to come.

"Mother!" said Ralph, coming to the door of the drawing-room, his dressing only half finished, "will you grant us a favour to-night?"

"Come, Ralph!" said his father, glancing up from the pages of the weekly paper, and smiling at the lad's happy expression, "you are going to ask something terrible, I know, otherwise you would never begin in that way!"

"What is it, my boy?" asked his mother.

"We are so tired of wearing collars, mother. They are so uncomfortable in hot weather, and they make us feel as though we were at school, you know. Can we leave them off for supper, and wear handkerchiefs round our necks instead?"

I doubt if Mrs. Everdale could have refused even a more serious request than that on the first evening of her boy's return, and so with a look and a smile that Ralph well understood she gave assent, and that young gentleman returned to his room, performing on the way an exaggeration of a native dance. When he and Ernest came in at last Mr. Everdale was amused to see that they had adorned their necks with a white silk handkerchief each, fastened by a ring. It was a style affected by a rather fast class of young bushmen, and was therefore all the more ridiculous when used by these two lads. So long as they did not follow their models beyond that limit there was no harm likely to befall them.

It was late before any of them went to bed, there was so much to be talked of. Mr. and Mrs. Everdale wanted to know everything about the school and the friends they had made; and on their side the boys had hundreds of questions to ask about favourite horses, about shooting, hunting, black fellows, and other things of similar importance. The little party sat out in the verandah enjoying the cool night air; at least, Mr. and Mrs. Everdale sat, but the boys walked about, lay down or sat down, just as the inclination seized them.

"Oh, I say, father!" exclaimed Ralph; "what about that white kangaroo? Is it still about the run, or has it been caught?"

"No! it is still here. I think the men have tried to run it down several times since you were here last, but it manages to get away from them, and the blacks have thrown spears and waddies at it in vain. Sambo is feeling quite nervous about it, and says that it is bewitched."

"Well, it is curious how it escapes so often. But Ern and I will put an end to the mystery before we go back to school: you see if we don't. Won't we, Ern?"

"I should rather think so! If we can't run it down—well, we shall be ashamed to go back to school again, that's all!"

"I am sure you would!" said Mrs. Everdale; "and as it is necessary that you do go back, I trust that you will succeed in catching this wonderful kangaroo."

The evening passed quickly away in pleasant talk, the boys laying numberless plans for future deeds. Then the servants came in, a chapter was read, prayers said, and the household retired to rest. All the windows and doors were left wide open, and into the room where the boys slept the moonlight streamed with full radiance.

CHAPTER III.

WILLAROO

WHILE everybody is fast asleep I shall try to describe the appearance of the station. It lay many hundreds of miles to the north of Adelaide, and was a very quiet place to live at. The nearest village, or, as they are generally called in Australia, township, was eighty miles distant, but it might have been double that for all the good it was in the matter of supplying society to Mr. and Mrs. Everdale; for, counting every building in the place, there were not more than twenty, and these were chiefly occupied by tradesmen, mechanics, and labourers. There were the homesteads of other squatters, to be sure, where men and women of the Everdales' class lived, but as the nearest of these was more than forty miles off, visiting was not a common occurrence. But once or twice a year three or four of the neighbouring squatters made a point of going to each other's homes and staying for a few days at a time. This life had been a great change to the one the Everdales had led in England, and to Mrs. Everdale especially it had for a time appeared very dull and monotonous, but that feeling had worn off, and she had learned to be content. They had had several other children, but these had gone one by one to the "House of many mansions," until Ralph only was left to cheer and comfort them.

But beyond all this there was the change of climate and the seasons, and the different aspect of the country. The station was called Willaroo—the name given by the natives to the curlew *—and numbers of these birds frequented the plains. Mr. Everdale leased a considerable amount of land, and was the owner of fifty thousand sheep and ten thousand head of cattle. The house stood in a gully of a low range of stony hills, and close to the edge of a large creek. This was now quite dry, but in the winter time, when the rains were heavy, or after thunderstorms, it very often came down in a flood, carrying trees and logs and loose stones before it. The house itself was a big, rambling old place, built of wood from the floors up to the roof. The trees that grew upon the banks of the creek formed a pleasant background to it, but except these there were no other trees of any kind to be seen; the hills were quite bare of anything bigger than bushes.

* A species of bustard—not a water bird.

For many years it had been impossible to form a garden on account of the want of water, but the well just sunk would alter that. Already Mr. Everdale was having a piece of ground enclosed and dug about the house, and with the help of the water hoped to be able to grow plenty of flowers, and also—the greatest of all luxuries in the bush—vegetables. For the most part, potatoes were the only vegetable to be had at Willaroo from one year's end to another. So you may imagine how delighted everybody was at the thought of cabbages!

Besides the house in which Mr. Everdale lived, commonly known in bush parlance as "Government House," there were the kitchen and huts, where lived the men employed on the station. These were built away from the house, about a quarter of a mile further down the creek. Then there were the stables and stockyards, the carpenter's and blacksmith's shops under one roof, and last, but not least, the great wool-shed, where every year the sheep had their fleeces taken off by the shearers.

The big bell, hanging in the fork of a tree close to the kitchen, rang at six o'clock to call the men to work every morning of the week, with the exception of Sunday, when it rang only twice in the day for service at Government House. But Ralph and Ernest needed no bell to call them on the morning following their return home. Early rising was not a favourite practice of theirs, and at school they delighted to lie in bed until the very last minute; and I dare say they would not have awoke so early on this morning had it not been that the sun came streaming in through the open window right upon Ralph's face. Ernest was still fast asleep, but his cousin, having wetted the sponge at the wash-hand stand, threw it with unerring aim at his face, and then ducked down under the bed-clothes, feigning to be asleep.

But Ernest was not to be imposed upon by a pretence so transparent. He didn't mind the wet sponge in the least, it was not unpleasant on so hot a morning, but he determined to be revenged upon Ralph. Slipping out of bed as noiselessly as possible, he grasped his pillow and crept across the floor, meaning to give his cousin a good taste of it; but Ralph, sleeping like a cat, with one eye just a wee bit open, was too quick for him. He sprang up brandishing his pillow on high, standing on the bed, and showered down a rain of blows upon his antagonist. Then the fight became vigorous, and inclined first in favour of Ralph and then of Ernest. It was lucky that the pillow-cases were strong, or they must have come to grief in a very short time. Which of the two combatants would have been the victor I am not prepared to say, they were so well matched; but the heat, even at that early hour, caused them to call a truce and sink down upon their beds, hot with the exertion. The pause, however, was not of long continuance; the thought of the bath occurred to them at the same moment, and as a result they raced down the verandah at the top of their speed. .

After their bath dressing was a matter of a few moments only; counting each sock and boot they only had six articles of clothing to put on—a coat was not to be thought of until breakfast-time, and their hair had been cut so close to their heads that there was really no use in brushing it.

The men had not yet come up from their breakfast, and this fact suggested a brilliant idea to Ralph. He told it to Ernest, who grinned and nodded his head in assent, and both ran off to the kitchen. The bell-tree was at the back of the hut, and to this the boys went. Grasping the rope, they rang such a peal as would almost have roused up the dead horses and bullocks whose bones lay about the run bleaching in the sun. It didn't do that, but it did cause the men to rush out of their hut with alarm. They had not heard the bell rung in that way since the night upon which the store at the back of Government House had caught fire, and they wondered what could now be the matter. They ran round the end of the hut, treading on one another's heels in their

haste, and then stopped short as they caught sight of the two boys

They understood at once, and grinned at each other at having been misled.

"Good morning, gents!" said old Bill Stevens, a man who had been on Willaroo from the time when Ralph was a baby; "we heard a ring at our front-door bell, and came round to see who was honouring us with a call!"

"Thank you, Stevens," answered Ralph, with assumed gravity. Then drawing himself up and making his voice as manly as he possibly could, he said, "The work to-day my lads, will be as follows:—You, Stevens, will go out and bring in a good fat bullock, a white one, and have it killed; I am in want of a good stock-whip, and white will look best, I think."

"Your honour has but to speak, and 'tis done," replied old Stevens, without moving a muscle of his face, though his eyes were twinkling with fun.

"And you, Brown," addressing another of the men, "will get in those two chestnut colts—you know the ones — and break them in, so that my cousin and I can ride back to school before the holidays come to an end—if we wish to."

"That's one for you, Brown," said another man, named

Thompson Brown was one of the worst horsemen upon the run, and would have as soon tried to ride a flash of lightning as to get upon an unbroken colt.

"And you, Thompson." continued Ralph, knowing very well the excessive tenderness of this man's disposition, "will get in and kill as many sheep as will give a dish of kidneys for my breakfast."

The laugh was against Thompson this time.

Ralph's imagination was failing him now, and he turned away to go back to the house; but old Stevens had a word to say. He didn't see why he should not have his little joke.

"Oh. Mr. Ralph, sir," touching his hat, a thing that no man in Australia, especially in the bush, ever thinks of doing seriously; "if you please, sir, I should like a cheque for my bit of wages. I'm a-thinking of walking in to Adelaide to-morrow just for a holiday."

This bit of absurdity, seeing that Adelaide was several hundreds of miles away, was quite equal to any that Ralph could make up, so with a laugh and an "All right, Stevens," he and Ernest ran off. and the men returned to their breakfast. But these boys were just as careless and thoughtless as so many of their age are. Before they reached the house they met Mr Everdale.

"What was the bell ringing for so loudly?" he asked; and when they had told him, he said, "Fun is all very well in its way, and I like it myself when no harm can follow it; but you must have surely forgotten what I told you last night about poor Smith."

The faces of the two lads fell in an instant! They *had* forgotten; but they recollected, now, that Mr Everdale had told them of this man lying sick upon his bunk in one of the huts. He had been injured whilst working amongst the cattle one day in the yard. He was now recovering, after having had a hard fight to regain his health; all that was necessary for him was to have as much rest as possible.

"Oh, father! I am so sorry," exclaimed Ralph.

"And so am I!" chimed in Ernest sincerely. "We quite forgot the poor fellow."

"Shall we go back and tell him so?" asked Ralph.

"Yes! come on!" Ernest replied, turning to retrace his steps.

"Wait awhile, boys. Don't go now; you can do so later on. Go during the day, when the other men are away; I dare say he will be feeling lonely, and glad of your company for a time. Your mother goes down every day, and I think he will soon be able to get about again. But think next time before you act; do so always, and you will make life much happier, probably, both to yourselves and to others. Come along now, we are going to have breakfast at half-past seven, for I have a long distance to ride, and it is now twenty minutes past."

CHAPTER IV.

'POSSUMS

THE boys' appetites had been sharpened by their early morning exertions, and they did full justice to a breakfast consisting of grilled mutton chops, cold ham, scones, and home-made bread and butter. Mr. Everdale wondered a little how they managed to eat so much, until he remembered his own feats in that respect when he was a boy.

"I am going out to the Twenty-mile Camp," he said, during the meal. "I want to see how the cattle are doing out there. You two," addressing the boys, "had better have a day at home; it will be a rest for you."

"That will be the best plan, I am sure," said Mrs Everdale "I have one or two things for them to do, if they don't mind doing them"

"We'll do anything you wish, aunt," replied Ernest quickly.

"Always with the understanding," added Ralph, "that you will not ask us to do anything we ought not to do, mother!"

"Well," she replied, "I can but tell you what I want, and you must judge if it be right to do or not. I hadn't the least idea that you had become so particular, Ralph dear. Do you think you might allow yourselves to hunt out some opossums that have taken up their quarters between the ceiling and the roof of our kitchen?"

"Oh, that will be jolly!" exclaimed both boys in a breath. "How long have they been there?"

"For some months now, and they make such a noise at night that Eliza and Jane cannot sleep. Not only that, but the other night one opossum fell down through a hole in the ceiling, which, as you know, is only of calico, right into Eliza's lap, as she was sitting at tea. It frightened her terribly."

"It must have done," said Mr. Everdale, laughing, "if we may judge by the scream she set up. Your mother and I rushed in, and there we found both the servants crowded into a corner of the kitchen, and the opossum, master of the situation, perched upon the mantelpiece. But I think it was just as much frightened as the women were."

"And did you kill it, uncle?" Ernest asked, much interested.

"No, that he didn't!" laughed Mrs. Everdale. "Your uncle armed himself with the poker, and went towards the mantelpiece; but just as he was about to kill the opossum it made a violent spring, landed upon your uncle's head, and with another jump from there got outside the door, and so escaped. Your uncle was almost as much frightened as the servants."

"My dear," said Mr. Everdale, "if you *will* tell tales out of school, it is only fair that I should tell the boys how, at the same moment, you ran behind the kitchen-door to hide yourself!"

Ralph and Ernest were immensely amused at this adventure, and began to discuss plans as to the best method of dislodging these harmless but unwelcome intruders.

"There is something else you can do also," said Mr. Everdale, who, having finished his breakfast, arose from the table. "Your riding horses will be in to-day, and will require to be shod; it is quite likely that, as they have been doing nothing for so many months, they will be restive; so you can help the blacksmith while he is shoeing them."

"If they are not too restless," added Ralph, "I'll get

Brown to let me put one of the shoes on. I shall soon be forgetting all he taught me before."

"Yes, you can do that; there is nothing like being able to help yourself. Oh, and there is another thing! I hear that some of our black friends and their families will be here to-day, and they will want some rations given to them. You boys can do that; you know how much to give them, and it will help your mother."

Saying this, Mr. Everdale went out, and the boys began to arrange for the siege of the opossums' stronghold.

"The first thing to do," said Ernest, with the gravity of a general on the eve of some action—"the first thing to do is to find out the exact position in the roof of our enemies. How shall we do that?"

"We'll go and ask Eliza; she'll know pretty well, I expect. It will be just the same as asking the people of a country the direction taken by an invading army."

Eliza was only too glad to give all the information of which she was possessed, and in a few minutes the boys had determined to begin the attack at one particular spot. To this they were further guided by signs found upon the roof. The roof consisted of wooden shingles nailed upon rafters, but some of the shingles had become loose and partly detached from their fastenings. One of these, just where the roof came down over the wall, had been pushed aside, and upon a projecting nail were some little bits of fluffy fur. A ladder had been obtained, and Ralph had mounted to the top. Ernest was one or two rungs lower down.

"We want a long stick now!" said Ralph; "hand me up one—quick, Ernest!"

There were plenty of long, slender saplings lying about the wood-heap, and in a minute or two Ralph was poking about in the dark hole he had found. For a while he was unsuccessful, but at last, in a corner, the stick pressed against something soft.

"Here they are!" called Ralph, in an excited tone, to Ernest.

"Poke them up then, and perhaps they will come out But are you sure you are right?"

"Quite sure. Listen now when I dig the stick in!"

There could be no doubt about it. As he worked the stick backwards and forwards a low, guttural snarl could be heard; the father of the family was evidently protesting against being disturbed in his daily sleep, and to make doubly sure Ralph pulled the stick back, and upon the end of it were signs of 'possum fur! No amount of prodding with a stick was of any avail—they simply snarled and stayed in their retreat. If instead of a kitchen roof they had been in the hollow limb of a tree, it would have been the simplest thing, for the boys would then have cut them out with an axe, or lighting a fire at one end of it, would have driven them forth with the smoke Of course, both of these plans were out of the question in the present instance. A council of war was held, Ralph sitting upon the ladder, Ernest standing at the foot looking up, his hands in his pockets and his legs far apart; and last, but by no means least, old Rover, the retriever dog. I had almost forgotten to mention him, but he was indeed as keen in this matter of 'possums as were his young masters.

He sat on the ground close to Ernest, sweeping the surface with his tail in ceaseless movement, his hot red tongue lolling out at one side of his mouth, and his eyes perfectly ablaze with excitement. He was an impatient old dog, and every few minutes he would rear up against the ladder as though longing to climb it, at the same time barking in a deep voice, which must have made the 'possums tremble in their hiding-place Mrs. Everdale had come out, partly to see as much of the boys as possible, and partly to see that in their eagerness they did not tear half the shingles off the kitchen. Ernest was the one to hit upon a solution of the problem.

"I'll tell you, Ralph, how we'll manage them! We'll tie a hook on to the end of the stick and fish them out!"

"In another moment came tumbling out a fine old 'possum; down he went off the roof

"Yes, that will do, perhaps," said Ralph, with just sufficient doubt in the tone of his voice to make it appear that *he* would have thought of a superior plan in two minutes more. "But where are you going to get a hook with a sharp point?"

"Why, a meat-hook will do capitally. Can I ask Eliza for one, aunt?"

It was given to him at once, and he began to fasten it on to the end of a stick. When this had been done he said, "Now, you'd better come down, Ralph, and let me have a try."

"There's no use doing that. Give me the stick, and I'll have them out in no time."

"That is likely, after my thinking of it, and getting the hook and everything! Come down!"

"It's too much trouble. I'm on the ladder, and I'm going to stay there. You are such a child, Ern; what does it matter who pulls the 'possums out? Come on, hand up the hook!"

"I'll hook you down with it, rather!" replied Ernest quickly. "You have had your try, and it's my turn now."

"That's all nonsense. I am the oldest, and I shall do what I like—so there!"

It is quite possible that from words these boys would

have proceeded to blows. As a rule, they were the best of friends, and would stand shoulder to shoulder in defence of each other in school scrimmages; but they both loved to have their own way, and would haggle and argue over a thing until they lost their tempers.

"Come, boys — or *children,* I ought to call you," exclaimed Mrs. Everdale, who had been listening to the argument; "it is ridiculous to behave in that way. Ralph, you are the eldest, and ought to set a good example; Ernest has certainly the right to take your place, seeing that you have been trying in vain for some time, and the hook is certainly his invention."

A word from his mother was always sufficient to bring Ralph to his senses at times such as these. He was himself again in a moment.

"All right, mother, if you think Ern ought to hook the 'possums, I'll hook it out of here. Only if he tumbles off the ladder and breaks an arm or two, don't blame me, please."

Ernest was climbing up almost before Ralph was on the ground. He thrust in the stick, groped about for a minute, and then shouted, "Look out!" There was a sound of scratching and snarling within the roof as he pulled the stick towards him.

Rover was watching him with fixed gaze and glistening teeth. Ralph was on the look-out, and Mrs. Everdale retreated behind the wood-pile.

In another moment came tumbling out a fine old 'possum; down he went off the roof right upon Ralph's shoulders. Rover sprang at it in a moment, and the suddenness of the two shocks sent the boy rolling in the dust. The 'possum got safe into the wood-heap, but was soon routed out, and then took to the open, hoping, perhaps, to get to the trees in the creek. But here Rover had the advantage over it, and in two minutes it had paid forfeit.

This success did away with all unpleasantness between the boys, and when Ralph took the hook and brought out the second opossum Ernest was quite content. Altogether they got four out of the roof, but none of the others afforded them as much sport as the first one.

CHAPTER V.

"*PEPPER.*"

The process of taking the skins off the 'possums occupied some time; then nails had to be found with which to peg them out to dry upon a tree. The boys had an idea of collecting sufficient to make a rug, and taking it with them to school as a specimen of their powers in hunting. At first, however, they were not sure how many would be necessary, but on counting the skins in a rug belonging to Mr. Everdale they found that at the very least they would have to kill from sixty to seventy opossums.

Just before the bell rang for the midday dinner they heard the crack of a stock-whip, and very soon afterwards the sound of horses galloping. This was the man bringing in from a distant part of the run the mob of horses in which were the two belonging to the boys. They ran to the yard to see that the gate was open, and then stood and watched the horses tearing along as fast as they could go.

A big black horse was in the lead, and set the others an example in kicking up his heels, neighing, plunging, and in other ways trying to show what a wonderful creature he was. Just as they came close to the yard this leader suddenly swerved away and galloped off, trying to escape, but the man who was driving them was too quick; putting spurs to his horse he went off in a slanting direction, so as to get ahead of the runaway, and then, having succeeded in stopping him, began to use the stock-whip.

Ralph and Ernest had brought a whip each with them from the stables, and now went into the yard to catch their horses. This was not an easy matter; they were not vicious, but the recent gallop had excited them and made them shy of being caught.

It was some time before Ralph could catch the one he wanted, and then only succeeded by chasing it into a smaller yard by itself. It didn't look very safe for these boys to be in a yard with forty or fifty horses running round and round them, but they had been used to it from childhood, and were quite unconcerned as to what the horses might do. The man who had brought the mob in was also the station blacksmith, and he now prepared for shoeing. All the horses on Willaroo had to have shoes, because, though there were no hard roads as in England, the ground is thickly covered with loose stones as big as hens' eggs.

While Ralph led his horse down to the blacksmith's shop, Ernest ran over to the kitchen for a fire-stick, with which to light the fire in the forge; he also took upon himself the office of bellows-blower, and very soon had the fire roaring and sending up showers of sparks Ralph had hoped to have done some portion of the shoeing himself; he had assisted the blacksmith many times, and had learned how to do it properly. But in this instance he had to stand by and look on, for his horse (whose name, by the way, was "Pepper") proved to be very restless and touchy. Master Pepper had had too long a holiday, and did not like the idea of being made to work. The blacksmith soon lost all patience with him, and at last had to tie a bandage over his eyes. This frightened him; not being able to look about and shy at everything, he stood still, and very soon had four new shoes nailed to his feet.

In the afternoon several black women and children arrived. They were the wives and families of a few partly civilised natives, who camped about the homestead at different times during the year. The men were hunting kangaroos and wallabies, and would not arrive until sundown.

The women walked one behind the other, and as is

the case with most savage races, they were the servants and beasts of burden to their lords and masters. They were dressed in all sorts and conditions of clothes, and a very curious appearance they presented. Some of the lubras* had a dirty cloth tied round their heads, others had no head-gear at all, but there was one who walked proudly along wearing a battered white beaver hat. It belonged to her husband, and was carried in this way so as to save it from being more crushed than it already was. Slung over their backs they had great big bundles containing all the goods they were possessed of, domestic and otherwise. Their cooking things for the most part were simply a tin pot and a tin dish. Through the strings that tied the bundles were stuck spare waddies, spears, and other weapons, and in most cases one or more babies were perched on top of all and hung on as best they could. The loads were heavy, and the women were bent almost double as they walked. In their right hands they carried a digging-stick. This was a piece of wood five feet long, one end rather broad and flat, and pointed and charred by fire to make it hard. The other end was rounded off to form a handle, and was notched and carved so as to give a better grasp to the hand. This is particularly a native woman's instrument, and is used

* L

for digging up roots, grubs, making holes, &c., and on occasion can be used as a weapon of offence or defence. In the present instance it was used as a walking-staff, and gave the natives somewhat the appearance of pilgrims.

Seeing Mrs. Everdale standing in the verandah, they came towards her, and throwing their loads upon the ground, squatted down cross-legged, after the manner of Turks and tailors.

CHAPTER VI

FRIENDLY BLACKS

SOME of the women in the group of natives assembled near the house were quite young, and their faces were comely, but the older ones were wonderfully ugly. There was one old lady in particular who, by her manner of speaking, and the respect shown her by the others, was evidently a person of distinction. Her native name was almost unpronounceable, but to the whites she was known as "Willaroo Fanny." Her colour was a lustreless black. Her nose, or rather that flattened-out piece of flesh which did duty for one, was rendered still more hideous by the result of a blow given to her by some sharp-edged weapon. Between her teeth she held a very short clay pipe, puffing vigorously away at it. In reply to Mrs. Everdale's inquiries she answered, speaking in a slow whine, "Berry well, missus, thank you How you been gettin' on this long time? No got 'em any 'bacca, missus, you give 'um bit?"

"I'll give you some by-and-by, Fanny. Where are all the others?"

"Out there!" Fanny explained, stretching her hand out fan-shape, and sweeping it from north to south in a comprehensive manner.

"Catching kangaroos and emus, I suppose?"

"Yes, berry good; me eat kangaroo. You give 'um flour, chugar, tea-leaves, for poor old black lubra, missus? Berry good man your husband, allus give black feller plenty of tuck-out; berry good man dat!"

This compliment was thrown in, in the hope of making Mrs. Everdale more than usually liberal in dealing out food.

"Look at that picaninny,* mother," said Ralph, pointing to one of the babies that had just been unrolled from the folds of a 'possum rug. "Why, it isn't black a bit! It's copper-coloured. That's not a black picaninny!" he said, speaking to old Fanny.

"Him only that a-way 'cause him's young. You see 'um this?" she asked, laying her finger upon a dark smudge the size of a child's hand that was to be seen on the baby's forehead.

Ralph nodded.

"Berry well, as picaninny grow big that one mark go

* Picaninny—child

all about 'um body eberywhere, and he be all the same black fellow then."

Willaroo Fanny was perfectly right. Every native child is copper-coloured when young, but it always has this curious smudge upon the forehead. It looks as though some one had smeared some dark dye upon it with the fingers, and as the child grows, this mark spreads gradually over the whole of the body.

Mrs. Everdale had been looking amongst the faces of the other lubras to see how many of them she recognised. A few were strangers to her, and she missed one old woman who had been accustomed to come to the station for many a year.

"Where is old Polly?" she asked.

A dead silence fell upon the group, and they looked down upon the ground. There was no look of sadness on their faces, but one of dislike and fear. Mrs. Everdale repeated her question, and addressed it to old Fanny, but she only shook her head and made marks on the earth with her fingers.

"Come, Fanny, can't you speak?"

"No good, missus, talk a-long o' that one—no good."

"Why? has she run away?"

There was again silence, until the question being repeated, Fanny said, glancing round about uneasily at the time, " Old woman tumble down—break a back."

By this she meant to express that old Polly was dead, and the reluctance shown in speaking of the event arose from the belief that death is caused by witchcraft or an evil spirit. They fear that if they mention the circumstance the same thing may happen to them. The natives will never make their camps at the spot where one of their tribe is known to have died. They shun the place for ever afterwards.

Mrs. Everdale talked with them a little while longer, and meanwhile Ralph and Ernest went to the store and brought them flour, tea and sugar, and also some tobacco. The women mixed the sugar and tea into one parcel, going on the principle that as they had to be mixed in the water there could be no harm in doing it beforehand. Then, seeing that they were not likely to get anything more just then, they shouldered their bundles and walked away to a spot about half a mile from the house and began to form their camp. Later on the men passed by, dressed in cast-off clothing of the whites, but none of them wore hats. A few of them were strong, wiry-looking men. Each one had five or six dogs at his heels, as lean and mangy curs as ever ran on four legs.

One of the men—Sambo by name—came over to speak

to Ralph and Ernest, whom he quickly recognised. He was a short, thick-set man; his face had rather a pleasant expression, though it would have been much better had it lacked the cunning look in the eyes and the heavy, overhanging forehead. He said "Good day" to Ralph in the softest of wheedling tones, and almost every word was accompanied by a cringing motion of his body. No matter what any one said to him, Sambo always agreed.

"Will this be a good night for 'possum shooting, Sambo?" Ralph asked.

"Oh, berry good, big one good," replied Sambo, without hesitation.

"Not so good, I think," said Ernest. "as to-morrow night."

"Oh, no, to-morrow night berry much better; I think so too!" Sambo grinned in his pleasantest manner.

"You old sinner, Sambo!" exclaimed Ralph, laughing. Sambo understood this to be a compliment, and grinned and bowed delightedly. "Well, we are going out to-night; will you come with us, Sambo?"

"Too much tired this time; walk a long way to-day; 'nother time berry good, I think. Cloud come up by'm-by, then moon no see where 'possum sit 'long a tree."

"Well, you needn't come if you don't like; we don't

want you. And we needn't take any tobacco with us, Ernest, as Sambo doesn't care about it."

"No, we'll give it to one of the others. They are not tired, I know!"

"Oh, you boys, too much plenty nonsense every time. Me only gammon, me no tired now, and berry good moon just now soon as sun go away. Which way you go? 'long a creek?"

"Never mind; Billy will help us, I know."

"Billy no good; him fool, never know where 'possum sit down Me know berry good place, plenty 'possum, berry small tree, berry soon shoot 'em. 'S'pose you fetch 'em bacco, me show you plenty 'possum."

Sambo urged this view of the question with great earnestness, coming close to the boys, as he spoke and lowering his voice to a confidential whisper.

CHAPTER VII.

RUMOURS OF WILD BLACKS.

Mr. Everdale did not make his appearance until late, but the boys would not hear of sitting down to tea till he came.

"This is something like home," he said, looking round upon the happy faces at the table. "It makes up for the disagreeables of a long hot ride to be lovingly welcomed. Well, boys," he said, after a while, "how have you spent your time? Quite tired of so quiet a life, I expect, and longing to get back to your noisy school."

The boys set up a laugh of derision at such an absurd idea, and then both at once began to relate their doings.

"Did our blacks say anything about wild blacks being in the neighbourhood?" asked Mr. Everdale, when the boys had finished their story.

"No," said his wife, looking alarmed, "not a word! Have you any reason to suppose they are about again?"

The distinction between "our blacks" and "wild blacks" was that the former were partly civilised and docile, and the latter, a different tribe altogether, were as the Ishmaelites, their hands being against everybody, and everybody's hands against them. This wild tribe lived in the country some distance north of Willaroo, and not unfrequently came south on marauding excursions. There had been occasions when these blacks had surprised and murdered white men living in outlying huts upon other stations. These were stockriders, whose business it was to see that the cattle did not stray too far away. It was the remembrance of these murders that made Mrs. Everdale feel alarmed at her husband's question.

"I am sorry to say," replied Mr. Everdale, in answer to his wife's question, "that I have very good reason to suppose so. In riding through a thick belt of scrub * we came upon a bullock that had been freshly speared and the greater part of the meat cut off the bones The marks of feet upon the ground showed that a number of blacks had been there."

"And hadn't the stockmen seen any of them about, father?" asked Ralph.

"No; they were as much surprised as I was. We

* Scrub—a mass of thickly-growing bushes and dwarfed trees Underwood.

have not had any bother with those fellows for some time now."

"Will it be necessary to go and chase them?" Ernest asked, rather hoping that his uncle would say yes, and perhaps allow Ralph and himself to go.

"No, I shan't go out against them just because they kill a bullock or two. We've taken away their hunting ground, and must not be surprised if they resent it sometimes. Of course, if they molest the men, that is a different matter. But our fellows have never ill-used them, so I think we need not fear them much."

"Those stockmen who were murdered on Pinga Station had ill-treated the natives, hadn't they, uncle?"

"Yes, most shamefully. I believe that having come suddenly upon some blacks busy slaughtering a beast, they ran one down and caught him; then they tied him to a tree, and almost cut the poor fellow to pieces with their stock-whips."

"What wretches!" exclaimed Mrs Everdale.

"I don't believe any of our men would do such a thing—do you, father?" said Ralph.

"I don't know, my boy, I hope not, I am sure. But you can't tell what people will do when their passions are aroused, and they have never been taught to curb them. However, I warned our fellows to be very cautious how they went about, and on no account to interfere with the blacks except in self-defence."

"Are they well-armed?" asked Ernest, referring to the stockmen.

"They have revolvers and carbines in the hut, but lately, not seeing any blacks about, they left off carrying them. But I have ordered them always to do so now, and also that they should ride in pairs. I trust nothing more serious than the loss of a few bullocks will happen."

Just then a low whistle was heard coming from some one outside. Ernest, being nearest the door, jumped up from his chair to see who it was. "It is Sambo," he said, coming back. "He wants to know, Ralph, if we are going out shooting to-night?"

"It is rather late, boys, isn't it?" suggested Mrs. Everdale, glancing at the clock, which was close upon the hour of nine. "Stay at home to-night, and we'll have some music and singing."

"Yes, that will be the thing!" said Mr. Everdale. "I haven't had any music for a long time. You never indulge me, my dear, in the same way you do these boys!"

"'Tis you that never play or sing to me, John. Considering that you can tune pianos, you ought to be the chief musician!"

It might be supposed that pianos were rare things in these far-away places in the Australian bush, but where ladies live, a piano, or at the least a harmonium, is almost certain to be found. It whiles away many a tedious hour by recalling scenes in the mother country, where "the old songs" were sung. Mr. Everdale's talent was exceptional, and had been called into play far and wide amongst his neighbours.

The boys were quite willing to do as Mrs. Everdale suggested, and tried to get rid of Sambo, but this they could not do until they had given him a piece of tobacco.

Then Mrs. Everdale played, while her husband smoked in the verandah, lying at full length upon a home-made lounge. The doors and windows of the drawing-room were open, and the tones of the piano floated out upon the air of the calm, moonlit night. Ernest lay upon the floor of the verandah. Ralph sat beside his mother, while the maid-servants came round the house where they could hear better, and even the men sauntered up and lay in the shadow of a big gum-tree.

CHAPTER VIII.

SMITH'S TWO FRIENDS

NEXT morning, after breakfast, Ralph and Ernest went down to the hut to visit the sick man. They had intended doing this on the previous day, but what with hunting 'possums, shoeing horses, cleaning guns, and talking to natives, they had quite forgotten their resolution. They found Smith sitting up in an armchair, which a handy man had made out of an old cask; it was nicely lined and padded, and was most comfortable. The invalid brightened up when he saw the boys enter. He could read, but did not care for it, tales did not seem real to him; he would have given all the books in the world had they been his to be able to spring into his saddle and gallop after wild cattle in the scrub. Since the day he had been able to leave his bed and sit in his chair he had found occupation in plaiting thongs for stock-whips. The boys found him busy upon an almost finished thong, and another quite completed hung upon a nail on the wall.

"Well, Smith, how are you getting on?" asked Ralph; "we've come to have a yarn with you, if you don't mind."

"Mind!" echoed the patient "Well, that isn't likely anyway, seeing how I'm cooped up here like a goose with a lame leg. I'm getting on fine now, sir, thank ye, and hope soon to feel Blueskin under me again. I expect the old hoss will be as fresh as a two-year old by this time! He won't be too fresh for me, anyway"

"There are not many horses able to throw you, are there?" asked Ernest, gazing with admiration at one of the best riders in the colony.

"Well, I won't say that, sir, 'cause it ain't safe to boast; you never can tell what's going to happen. But so far, I have mastered pretty well every hoss that I've put my legs over. As long as the tackling holds, I feel pretty certain of sticking on."

"But I've heard fellows say," remarked Ralph, "that they have sat their horse after he has bucked his saddle off!"

"Ah! they can tell that to the Marines, they can! I've seen some good riding, but I've never seen that done on a horse that's buck-jumping downright proper. Why, it stands to reason, that if a fellow has to use all his strength to stick to his saddle, he hasn't got much chance of stopping on the hoss's bare back."

"Those are capital whips you are making!" Ernest said, who had been watching the process of plaiting with great attention.

Smith was working sixteen strands, and to the boys it looked a confused tangle.

"I can't make out how you keep the whole lot going," said Ralph, "or how you manage to make the thong round instead of square."

"It's just practice, sir; a Mexican chap taught me: he was A1 at it. When I have done the plaiting, I am going to make the handles out of a fine piece of miall* I have under the bunk there. I am going to make the lower part where the hand takes it six-sided, and inlay it with malachite and mother-o'-pearl; then I shall run a pattern in between. made by pins' heads driven in."

"I say!" exclaimed the boys together, "what jolly stock-whips those will be!"

"Well, they won't be bad, if I can finish them to my liking. Another thing I am going to do is, to put

* Miall—a wood having a scent similar to raspberry jam, and very hard and well-grained.

the names of two friends of mine on the handles, and give the whips away."

"Your friends will be very proud of them, I know," said Ernest, secretly envying them the possession of these whips.

"Well, I hope so, I am sure. Ain't it curious now, that these two friends of mine are named Ralph and Ernest Everdale?"

Smith went on with his plaiting, his face as grave as that of a judge; but he glanced at the faces of the boys to see how they would take the announcement. I don't know for certain what effect he had hoped to produce, but if it was one of pleasure and surprise he was well repaid. Ralph and Ernest actually coloured with the suddenness of the surprise.

"Oh!" they gasped. "For us! Oh, Smith, you are good!"

"I'm sure we don't deserve them," said Ralph; "why, it was only yesterday morning that we rang the bell out there in a way that must have frightened you fearfully."

"It did give me a start for a moment," Smith replied, his face beaming with satisfaction at the success of his gift to the lads; "but as soon as I heard your voices and what you were saying I lay back and laughed to myself quiet like."

"But we have never done anything to deserve such a handsome present from you!" exclaimed Ernest, knowing that whip handles ornamented in Smith's best style were worth two pounds each; he had known that price to have been given for them several times.

"It is just this way," explained Smith. "It doesn't matter whether you deserve anything from me or not, though you've always treated me like gentlemen. But you see, in giving these things to you, I am trying to make up somehow for the kindness of the missus up yonder"—nodding in the direction of the house. "Every day she's been down here, and always had something pleasant to say to cheer a fellow up with. Why, she'd tell me more about what was going on in two minutes than the chaps in the kitchen could tell me in an hour! And one day she came down on purpose to tell me that she had seen old Blueskin, and that he was doing well! Now that's what I call something like!"

"Mother *is* just the best woman in the world!" asserted Ralph, warmed up to a pitch of enthusiasm by Smith's quaint praise. "But ladies on other stations would do just the same if you were laid up there"

"Don't you believe it, sir, because I know better. I've had a little experience of it. Now Mrs. Everdale *is* downright pious, and no mistake! but she doesn't keep putting it into words; you can feel it, and that's the kind of religion that does a chap good. More than once she made me feel that I was an uncommon ordinary fellow, and it isn't often I felt that way, I can tell you, and I'm not going to forget her kindness anyhow, so you must take these whips as a sort of return from me to her."

It was a new experience to Smith to make a confession such as this, and he spoke quickly and with a curious shamefacedness of expression. As soon as he had got through with it he began to talk of other matters, and in a little while the boys left him.

CHAPTER IX.

"THE SHAKING" MALLEE TREE.

THEIR strangest adventure—or, in fact, the only thing that, so far, had happened to them worth calling an adventure—occurred in the afternoon. They had ridden out with the intention of hunting kangaroos, and also to take a message from Mr. Everdale to one of the men living out on the run. The only things they carried with them were a tomahawk * slung to Ralph's saddle by a leather holder similar to those used by firemen, and a canvas bag of water; this was slung by straps to Ernest's saddle, and lay against his horse's side. The bag of water was certainly a necessary thing in hot weather and a dry country, but even the boys would have had difficulty in explaining to what use they expected to put the tomahawk.

Old Rover was chained up, as being too old for fast work, but they took another dog with them, of a kind especially adapted for hunting.

* Tomahawk—a small hatchet

The way lay through stony hills for some distance. To any one unaccustomed to bush-horses and bush-riders, it would have appeared impossible to gallop over such rough country. But these lads thought nothing of it. They went off at full speed as soon as they started a kangaroo, and their horses seemed to enjoy the fun as much as their riders. They shot down the hills, over rocks and loose rolling stones, with the sure-footedness of goats. They required no urging with spur or whip, but entered thoroughly into the spirit of the thing. It was certainly as good as cattle mustering.

The dog, however, met with an accident. A large red-skinned kangaroo had been started, one that is commonly known as an "old man," and at the time Ralph had called to Ernest that he was certain the kangaroo would not go far before "sticking up" and showing fight. This proved to be the case, for very soon the "old man" faced suddenly round, and sitting erect upon his hind legs he showed a bold front to his pursuers. From a distance it might have been supposed that he was sitting upon a three-legged stool, his tail supporting him behind, and so making the third leg.

The dog was close upon him, and being young and inexperienced, rushed straight for the throat of the kangaroo. In an instant the "old man" had enfolded him with his two short, strong fore-arms, and hugged him so tightly that the dog was forced to let go his grasp of the kangaroo's throat and yelp from pain. Then the "old man" lifted up one of his hind claws and with a vigorous and quick movement made a deep scratch down the dog's body. It would certainly have gone hard with him if help had not been close at hand; but the boys galloping up made the kangaroo drop him and try to run away. Badly hurt as he was, the dog was not going to allow his enemy to be the victor, and in a moment seized him by the haunch and threw him down. Then it became a rough-and-tumble fight between dog and kangaroo, both giving and taking nasty wounds.

By this time Ralph had dismounted and had given his horse to Ernest to hold. Taking a stout stick he ran to assist the dog. The "old man" came at him at once, and tried to get him within his arms. Ralph made a blow at his head and missed, but at that moment the dog made a fresh assault from the rear, and against enemies on both sides the kangaroo was unable to contend. Jumping round to shake off the dog, Ralph had a chance to get in another blow; he brought the stick down just between the kangaroo's ears and killed him. The "old man" had made a plucky fight, however, and the dog bore evidence of the sharpness of his claws.

Ralph bound one or two of the worst ones up with strips of pocket-handkerchief, but they had no more hunting on that afternoon. They rode quietly along to the stockman's hut, gave their message, rested their horses for half-an-hour, and had some tea without milk, and a piece of cake made of flour, fat, and sugar, commonly known as browny" Then they tightened their girths and turned their horses' heads homewards.

The hut they had just left lay in a northerly direction from the station, not far off the route that Mr Everdale had travelled the day before. The probability of seeing traces of wild blacks had suggested itself to the minds of the boys, and they had asked the stockman if he had seen any signs of them. It seemed that he had seen tracks, but could not say whether they belonged to the wild or to the station tribe. A cart-track led from the hut to the homestead, but, in order to avoid a patch of thick scrub, it went round about, and thus made the distance to be travelled some two or three miles further.

Knowing this part of the country perfectly, the boys determined to strike across country to save time, and very soon had entered the scrub. This was formed of large bushes of acacia, and a stunted description of gum-tree known as mallee. Small bushes of different kinds and fallen trees made the undergrowth very thick, and the horses had to wind in and out to find a way through.

All at once the boys heard the dog bark; the sound came from the right, and looking in that direction they saw a curious sight. Some twenty yards distant the head of a mallee showed above the surrounding acacias, but the strange thing was that this tree was seen to shake violently every now and then.

"What can it be?" said Ralph, reining in his horse.

"I don't know! Let's go and see. Look, it has stopped shaking now!"

"No, there it goes again; and it is there the dog is barking. Come on, we'll find out"

"Very likely it is a kangaroo hung up by the leg; it may have been trying to reach the leaves, and has got fast in the fork of a branch."

"Stuff! Kangaroos don't eat mallee leaves when they can get better food. Now, then, Pepper, old fellow, what's the matter?"

This exclamation was caused by the horse shying violently away from the spot they were approaching. Ralph could see nothing except the tree shaking violently, but the horse having its eyes nearer the ground could evidently see something through the bushes that frightened it. Ernest's horse behaved in the same way, and refused to go forward another step, but copied Pepper in snorting and shying in the most absurd manner. And all the time the dog kept on barking in a way that made the boys think he had got some animal at bay; it was a worrying bark.

Every now and then they could hear a series of curious guttural sounds, but what was causing them they could not imagine. It was evidently no use making further efforts to get their horses forward, for not an inch would they move except sideways or backwards.

Ralph and Ernest were greatly excited by this time, but not at all frightened; they knew that there were no savage animals in the country, but had no idea of the real state of the case. They now dismounted and tied the horses up to a bush, and Ralph unslung his tomahawk—'In case," as he remarked, "of accidents' They were about to discover how peculiarly fortunate it was that the tomahawk had been brought.

Pushing their way through the bushes they came out on a clear space, in the centre of which was the shaking tree. They suddenly stopped as they beheld the cause, and uttered a cry of astonishment.

Ernest and Ralph were astonished—and no wonder—for, hanging head downwards from the tree, they saw the form of a black fellow. One foot was caught in the fork of a branch, and so high up that only the man's head and shoulders touched the ground.

The boys quickly recovered from their surprise, and rushed forward to give assistance to this unfortunate man. At first they tried to raise him bodily, but the weight was too great for their strength.

"The tomahawk!" exclaimed Ernest. "We must cut the tree down!"

Ralph had picked it up almost before Ernest had finished speaking, and was hacking at the trunk with tremendous energy. The stem was not very thick, and in a short time was cut through and fell over. And now a thing happened which might have been foreseen had the boys not been so hasty in carrying out their plan. The tree fell away from the man, and his foot being fixed, he was suddenly jerked forward with a good deal of force. The wrench to his leg must have been great, for he uttered a howl of pain; his head struck the stump of the tree, which stunned him.

"We have killed him in trying to save his life!" exclaimed Ernest.

"What donkeys we were! We might have cut the

limb that held his foot. Perhaps he isn't dead, though; let's look."

He wasn't dead, of course; it takes something more than a crack on the head to kill a native. Their skulls appear to be as hard as iron. He was simply stunned, and when Ralph saw this he ran to where the horses were standing, and brought the water-bag. The man's mouth was closed, and Ernest was obliged to open it with the pointed end of a waddy, one of the black fellow's weapons. His mouth was opened now, and Ralph tilted the bag up to pour some water into it. His hand shook, perhaps, or the water came more quickly than he expected, but, whatever the cause, out it came in a gush right in the black fellow's face. But the effect produced was instantaneous. The man gave one great gasp for breath, then sneezed, opened his eyes, and sat up.

Long before this the boys had recognised him as being a member of the wild tribe, and though they had not expressed their thoughts in words, they both wondered if he would try to kill them or run away with them.

It was this thought that prompted Ralph, as soon as the black sat up, to pick up the tomahawk, and place it in a convenient position through his belt. "If," he thought, "the fellow has no gratitude, and means to return evil for good, he shan't have it all his own way, if I know it; I'll get a chop at him somehow."

But the man had some good feelings in his heart, and though he could not express himself at all clearly in words, he yet made his gratitude understood by signs. He knew a few words of English, though where he could have learned them the boys did not know, but he repeated them over and over again, grinning and nodding his head at the same time.

It was impossible to tell for how long he had been fixed in the tree, but judging from the size of the hole scraped in the sandy soil where his head and shoulders had rested, he must have been there for many hours at least. The skin was rubbed off his ankle where it had chafed in his continued struggles to get free. If he could have understood them, the boys longed to ask why he had climbed the tree. They had now done all that was in their power to help him, and it was time to go home. The native appeared to be very stiff as he rose to gather his spears and waddies together, and he limped on his injured leg as he walked away.

CHAPTER X.

SPORT AT NIGHT.

This incident gave the boys plenty to talk about all the way to the station, and an exciting story to tell at the tea-table

Mr. Everdale would hardly believe it at first. "Well," said he, "it was a most fortunate thing you found him. We should be apt to call it chance if we did not know of a Higher Power that orders everything to one great end That one act of kindness may do wonders with that wild tribe."

"I hope," said Ralph, "that it will make them more particular about spearing our cattle and killing the stockmen. We shall have done good to-day if that is the effect."

"I should like to be a missionary when I am older," Ernest said thoughtfully, "and go out amongst those black fellows. I expect they could be taught"

"They'd kill you before a week was out, and make charms from bits of your bones."

"I'd risk that for their good, though I believe that if one went amongst them unarmed and showed trust in them, they would not hurt one."

"'Tis a noble idea, Ernest," Mrs. Everdale said, glancing at the boy's face as it brightened with the glow of enthusiasm "When the time comes for you to leave school and choose a calling in life, I shall hope to see you with the same faith The natives deserve better treatment from the whites than they at present get."

"I shall be a squatter, the same as father is," said Ralph; "and then I can help Ern with money, and clothes, and horses; and if the blacks kill him I'll get a party together and go out and avenge his death two or three times over!"

"What a horrible idea, Ralph!" interposed his mother. "You would do away at once with all the good that Ernest may take years, perhaps, to accomplish."

"Well, of course, mother, I wouldn't think of doing such a thing just because the blacks killed a few bullocks, or even stockmen, that one did not know very well; but I think I'd do it if they killed Ernest."

"You are talking about what you do not understand,"

said his father, rising from the table. "I know that you feel a strong affection for Ernest, but if you think over the precepts of our Master you would see that you would be committing a grievous wrong. We would hope that Ernest would be preserved in his good work; but, in any case, we must leave the punishment of such evil deeds in the hands of God."

Ralph was silent. What he had already said was as much in jest as earnest, and seeing that his father had taken it seriously he would say no more.

Soon after tea Sambo came to see if the boys intended to go out 'possum hunting. There was nothing to stop them to-night, and in a short time they set out. Ralph and Ernest each had a gun; Sambo had three or four small waddies, used for throwing at game, and a tomahawk; old Rover, glad to be off his chain, kept them company. The moon had not yet risen, but could not be far off, as the eastern sky was golden-coloured with her light. As they walked they discussed the question as to where was the best place to go, and decided to follow the creek until the moon rose sufficiently high in the heavens to be of service to them, and then they would work back towards home.

A better night could not have been chosen; the sky was without a cloud, and the moon when she appeared floated above in the full majesty of her beauty. The hunters followed the creek for a distance of three or four miles, and very weird and fairy-like was the scene. The gum-trees towered aloft to a great height, their white-barked trunks looking like regiments of ghosts starting up out of the deep shadows cast by the foliage. Here and there groves of the native pine were passed through, and where they grew thickly the light of the moon could not penetrate. It was rough walking, for the ground was stony; and, moreover, there were numberless short stumps of trees that had been cut down for timber, and against these the boys constantly stumbled.

By the time they turned to come back the moon was well up. Rover, who had been very busy sniffing round every tree he came to, was ordered to "Go find them," and in a few minutes he told by his bark that he had understood the order and had also carried it out.

On following the sounds of the dog they found him jumping up against the trunk of a tree. This was a sure sign that a 'possum was amongst the branches somewhere, but though all three peered into them nothing could be seen. Then they had to go through the process known as "mooning." Walking backwards from the tree, each one tried to get the various limbs

and branches between him and the moon, and then follow them out to the uttermost bunch of leaves where the 'possum might be feeding. This took up some time, and the constant looking upward made the neck ache; and there were other inconveniences, such as falling backwards over some fallen log or big stone. This process was continued for some minutes in silence; at last Sambo called out, "Me got 'um! Berry fine feller, right up there!"

Ralph reached the spot first, and following the direction of Sambo's finger as he pointed was soon able to detect the 'possum. It looked like a round, fluffy ball at first, the fur shining like silver along the ridge of its back, where it stood up against the light of the moon. Ralph raised his gun and fired; he had aimed well, and the 'possum came down with a tremendous "flop" upon the ground. Rover was waiting for it open-mouthed, but the boys beat him off, as his teeth would have damaged the fur. That was number one, and Sambo having put it into a net hanging across his shoulders, a fresh one was looked for. They soon found one. Ernest was the first to see it, and fired. The tree was high and the 'possum nearly at the top of it; that the shot had taken effect was evident, for the animal fell from the branch on to a lower one and there it hung suspended by the tail, dangling head downwards in the air.

"No hit him hard 'nough that time!" said Sambo. "Give 'um 'nother shot, Miss'r Ernest; him only picaninny dead."

This Ernest did, and brought it down.

It was late before they got home—quite two o'clock in the morning—and very tired the boys felt as they lay down in their beds. But they had had a good night's sport, having killed thirty 'possums. Their skins would go a long way towards the making of the proposed rug. Sambo had got his tobacco, and was quite satisfied with his share of the evening's sport, and old Rover had blissful dreams of 'possums who fell from the trees right into his mouth as soon as he barked at them.

The boys slept as soundly as tops, not waking until the bell for prayers sounded in their ears next morning. For an instant they fancied themselves back at school.

CHAPTER XI.

SUNDAY AT WILLAROO.

During the three or four days following the one upon which they found the black fellow hanging in the tree, the boys amused themselves in shooting, riding, playing cricket, or in any other way that presented itself. Cricket is a slow game with only two, so they pressed into their service the young black boys and as many of the older ones as cared to join. The blacks learned the game quickly, and became expert in blocking, or, when scouting, in stopping the ball. But they never made big hits when at the wickets, contenting themselves with making a sort of poking blow; neither would they attempt to make a catch when the ball was hit up.

When Sunday came it was kept as sacredly as possible, though it did happen occasionally that some work amongst the stock was left over from the week and had of necessity to be finished. On this Sunday, however there was nothing to hinder the Everdales from keeping it in the manner they considered right and proper. After breakfast the piano was wheeled into the dining-room, and chairs arranged for those of the men who chose to come to the reading of the service. At ten minutes to eleven a bell was rung, and at the hour the service began. The two maid-servants came, of course; cooking and all housework being reduced to the very smallest amount. Three or four of the men came, and on this particular Sunday, Smith, the stockman, came up leaning on the arm of a friend Then the service went on in its simple and beautiful language, and hymns were sung to tunes that were known to most of those present, and in which they heartily joined

The music, the devotional faces and attitudes of most of those present, and the pervading spirit of perfect rest and peace and simplicity, had an impressive effect upon men who in a large congregation in a church would have felt ill at ease and out of place. And there was one other thing that made them feel that religion was something more than an empty name, and that was the unvarying uprightness of conduct pursued by Mr. and Mrs. Everdale.

The day had come in with a dull, sultry heat; there was no wind, and the sensation felt by every one was as if they were being slowly stewed. Mr Everdale and others prophesied that a change of weather would soon take place, and that probably a thunderstorm would break forth before the day was at an end. And so it did. It was one of the heaviest that had come upon them for some time, and was very grand and terrible while it lasted. Louder and louder grew the thunder, and the lightning seemed to play about the room. Instinctively Mr. and Mrs Everdale and the boys drew closer together, and in silence watched the wondrous scene. They saw the blacks leave their wurleys* and run for shelter to a shed, where, cowering beneath their opossum rugs, they listened in terror to the thunder. It was a grand and awful sight, such as those who have not lived in southern latitudes can scarcely imagine. The lightning was incessant, flash following upon flash; the thunder one continuous roar and rattle, and distinct above all the sharp "swish" of the descending rain. It came quickly, and as quickly passed away; the sun rode in a cloudless sky, and every green thing washed by the rain glittered in the light; the blacks left the shed and wandered down to their wurleys to repair any damage that might have befallen them.

* Wurley—a rude shelter of boughs and leaves; very temporary, and of no use in rough weather

"The creek will come down soon, I expect," said Ralph.

"Certain to," answered Mr. Everdale; "and as the storm has travelled into the hills where it rises, it will probably come down very strongly."

"It will be worth looking at," said Ernest. "There will be a lot of driftwood and rubbish carried down with it."

And before an hour had passed their words were verified. The creek had been quite dry, and had looked more like an immense unmade road covered with stones. But now it might have been called a river. It was a hundred and fifty yards wide at the least, and still rising. A stream of muddy-coloured, foam-flecked water rushed along between the banks, bearing on its bosom a quantity of timber and rubbish, and the stones could be heard knocking together at the bottom. The Everdales walked down to the bank and watched it for awhile. These floods were not frequent, and in a dry country running water has an especial attraction

Just before nightfall Sambo came running up to the house in a state of excitement. Mrs. Everdale was sitting with her husband and the boys in the verandah enjoying the cool sweet air; she had been reading the Bible, and the book lay upon her lap.

"I say, missis!" Sambo exclaimed, his eyes big with the earnestness of his mission; "I say, Miss'r Everdale! you look out: big feller water come along creek; berry big now, bigger by'm-by! Him come out all along house; you all be drowned: 'spose you run away long a-hill!"

"There's no danger, Sambo; this fellow-house stand too high, no water come here. We no run away."

"No use you talk like a-that, I know all about this one creek; him get berry big feller some time! You clear out quick or you sorry 'nother time!"

"Don't be afraid, Sambo," said Mrs. Everdale. "There will be no flood to drown us; this Book"—laying her hand on the Bible—"tells us so!"

Watching him as he went away, they saw him mount upon the stump of a tree and look steadily at the flooded creek. He was still there when night hid him from view.

"You did not convince him, mother," said Ralph, "he is evidently going to see if the creek is rising. If it does, I expect he will come rushing up again to have another try to persuade us to move."

"Well, it shows that he has some affection for us, poor fellow! He has been one of the most useful of the natives about here."

"That he has!" said Mr. Everdale. "He is really a good fellow."

At that moment a tap was heard at the door; Sambo was there, having come noiselessly on his bare feet. All his excitement had left him, but his face expressed great wonderment.

"Missis!" he said to Mrs. Everdale, "whereabouts that feller book tell you no flood come?"

Mrs. Everdale opened the Bible at the place and showed him. He could not read a word, but bending down till his face was close to the page he looked at it most intently for some moments in silence. Then he stood up, and putting his hand gently on the place, said, "My word! him berry good Book that; him know everythin'! Missis, next time you tell 'um me that Book say, 'No flood,' me say, 'Berry well, Sambo believe 'um.' Berry fine Book that!"

And then he went away. But the Everdales talked of little else but Sambo for the rest of the evening.

CHAPTER XII.

OFF TO THE OUT-STATION.

On Monday, Mr Everdale told the boys that he had to go to an out-station forty miles away to do some work amongst the cattle, and if they liked they might go with him. They jumped at the offer at once. Cattle mustering was quite as exciting as kangaroo hunting, and the possible danger attached to it added to their enjoyment

Mr. Everdale expected to be away for ten days or a fortnight; but as it would have been unkind to leave Mrs Everdale by herself for so long, it was settled that the boys should return after two or three days. They were to leave Willaroo on Wednesday morning early, and during the intervening time Ralph and Ernest were in a state of restless excitement and longed for the hour to arrive. They examined the feet of their horses to see if their shoes were in perfect order; looked to the girths of the saddles to be certain they were in good repair, and likewise overhauled their bridles from one end to the other. There would be some rough riding after the cattle, and the sudden breaking of a girth or the giving way of a buckle might prove serious. Hobbles* had to be looked up and well greased, and rugs and quart pots† selected, for they would have to camp out, and these things were necessary. They were made happy, indeed, when they found in the store two quart pots that had been in use, and, consequently, were as black as black could be. To have these slung to their saddles was far better than to have brand new ones, because it suggested the idea that the boys were in the habit of camping out, and had blackened the pots from constant use. Another reason why a black pot was to be preferred to a clean bright one was, that the black one would come sooner to the boil. There was, however, one important part of the outfit of a stockman which they did not possess, the lack of which rather damped their spirits, and that was a stock-whip. To ride after cattle without a whip was very much the same as going out shooting without a gun.

* Hobbles—straps linked together by a chain, and put upon the fore-legs of horses to keep them from straying.

† Quart pots—used for making tea when travelling. A tin cup form the lid.

Ralph said that the best way to solve the question was to go down and see Smith; this they did on the instant, and on entering his hut saw that their fears were groundless. The thongs were finished, and more than that, they were being fastened on to plain handles.

"I'd heard that you was going out, and knew you would want whips, so I buckled-to last night and got the last one finished. Of course the swell handles they ain't done, but these plain ones will answer the purpose just as well."

The boys were profuse in their thanks to Smith for his thoughtfulness.

"Now the next thing is," said Smith, "to see how you can handle them. I know that you have used whips now and again, but, if you'll excuse me saying so, you haven't quite got the knack. I'll come to the door and look on."

The boys were delighted to get a lesson from an expert, and were very soon practising as energetically as possible. It is by no means an easy matter to use one of these whips, with their immensely long lashes and short handles; and when a person first tries, he only succeeds in bringing the double of the thong across his face or round his legs, and in either case he gets a very unpleasant blow. Of course Ralph and his cousin were sufficiently familiar with the use of them to avoid these mishaps, but as Smith remarked, "A man who knows what he's about ought to be able to pick a fly off the ear of a sleeping bullock without waking him. I'll just see what I can do to show you what I mean, though I fear that my ribs won't let me have fair play. Now, you see this sixpence?"—throwing it out on the ground in front of him. "I'll show you how to pick it up."

Measuring the distance with his eye, Smith advanced a step forward, and with a swift cut with the whip caused the sixpence to fly towards him. He caught it in his left hand. Turning to the boys with a look of conscious pride, he suggested that they should try to do the same thing. But though they struck close to the spot, and even hit the sixpence itself. they could not make it come to them.

The next feat that Smith did was to cut the neck from a bottle standing on end, and the top from a young tree growing near the hut. Then he showed them how to make the heaviest blow possible with a stock-whip, and how to bring it down so as to make the loudest report with the cracker. He also told them that they must learn to use it in either hand,

and to pass it quickly from one hand to the other, standing in their stirrups. He had two eager pupils, and during the rest of the day they did little else but put his precepts into practice.

Wednesday morning came at last, and, after an early breakfast, Mr. Everdale, Ernest, and Ralph saddled their horses, and brought them across to the house to strap the rugs to the saddles. They had one rug a-piece, rolled tightly into a long, bolster-like form; and this was placed upon the pommel of the saddle, and, hanging down on either side, was fastened with straps. Their quart pots and hobbles hung on the left side, behind the saddle flap, and their stock-whips on the right, ready to their hands.

The weather was too hot to allow of coats being worn, so these were strapped on with the rug. Everything was soon ready for a start, and nothing more was to be done except say good-bye to Mrs. Everdale.

"When can I expect you two boys home again?" she asked, giving them a parting kiss. "I shall feel so lonely while you are away!"

"We'll come home on Saturday, mother, so you must try and keep your spirits up for three whole days. It won't be so bad as if we were off to school, you know."

"Shall I stay and keep you company, aunt?" asked Ernest, quite ready to do as he proposed.

"No, certainly not, my dear! I wouldn't spoil your enjoyment for so selfish a consideration on any account. As Ralph says, it is only for three days. But, Ralph," Mrs. Everdale continued, half playfully, "I hope you'll take an example of unselfishness from Ernest; you see he was ready to give up his ride to comfort me!"

"Why, of course," answered Ralph, the irrepressible; "isn't he going to be a missionary? And those are the sort of things he must do—saint-like, you know. But I'm going to be a squatter, and so, of course, must go about with father and learn how to muster cattle and all that sort of thing."

"I am sure I cannot see why a squatter should not be as unselfish as a missionary, Ralph; that is, if he wishes to act up to the highest standard set for us. You are a thorough boy for talking first and thinking afterwards." It was Mr. Everdale who spoke; and then, turning to his wife, he said, "Don't be alarmed if the boys do not come home on Saturday. It is just possible that I may want them to stay a day or two longer; they will be of assistance, because I am short-handed."

"That means that I am not to expect them until I see them!" answered Mrs. Everdale, smiling.

Then she bid them "good-bye," and watched them ride away. Just before they crossed the creek the boys looked back and waved their hats to her, and then they were lost to sight amongst the trees.

CHAPTER XIII.

THEIR FIRST KANGAROO.

The ride of forty miles was performed without anything happening on the way worthy of mention. They called at the hut of a stockman for food, and were there joined by a man from another part of the run. A little time after sunset, while it was yet light, the party arrived at the spot where they proposed to stay for the night.

The first thing to be done was to unsaddle the horses, hobble them, and turn them out to graze. Every man attended to his own horse, from Mr. Everdale downwards. Then a fire was lighted, and the quart pots being filled with water from a spring hard by, were placed round the fire to boil. Some interest was excited on the question being raised whose pot would boil first, and the boys and one of the men tried to win by raking the fire closer to their pots, and feeding it with small sticks. As soon as the water was boiling furiously, each man took a pinch of tea from the bag—the size varying with his taste for a strong or weak brew—and threw it into the pot, immediately covering it with the pannican, or tin cup, to keep the steam in. Sugar was added later on, but milk there was none. The food consisted of a round of salt beef and loaves of bread; the men cut lumps from them, and then, taking up their pots, sought seats on logs round about. As the night was sultry the fire was allowed to burn low, and the men, spreading their rugs upon the ground, lay a little distance from it and smoked their pipes and discussed plans for to-morrow's work, or told stories relating to their adventures in the bush.

The night was dark, the moon not rising till very late, or, more properly speaking, till very early in the morning, and the group around the fire formed a quaint picture. Not far away could be heard the jingling of the hobble chains and the tinkle of the bells, as the horses moved about in search of food, and now and then a curlew would whistle mournfully. When songs had been sung and more pipes smoked, it was time to turn in—though the hour was not later than nine o'clock—for they meant to rise at daybreak to begin work. Mr. Everdale and the boys did not forget to offer up thanks to Him who had protected them through the past day; then, scraping the stones and sticks away from under the blankets, and taking their saddles for pillows, the little party wrapped themselves in their rugs and fell asleep.

At the first break of day Mr. Everdale aroused the boys. They jumped up quickly when they saw the daylight, and giving one vigorous shake did all the dressing that was necessary. Two men went away to bring the horses up, and another lighted the fire, while the boys filled the quart pots at the spring and put them on to boil Breakfast was simply a repetition of supper, and was soon eaten. Then the rugs were rolled up and strapped to the saddles, and all mounted. Ralph and Ernest, in company with one man, rode in one direction, Mr. Everdale took a different one, the object being to muster or collect all the cattle off a certain piece of country and take them to a place where there were yards suitable for doing the necessary work.

Both the boys were thoroughly tired when towards evening they drove their mob of cattle up to the yard. It had been a long day certainly, but they had had some capital gallops after stubborn bullocks that would persist in going th wrong way. There were fewer songs that evening, and the hour of going to bed was earlier than on the previous night.

Friday was spent in the same way, and in the evening Mr. Everdale told the boys that they had better go back to the station in the morning; there was no reason, he found, for them to stay out longer. They would have preferred to help at the cattle-mustering until it was finished, but they obeyed Mr. Everdale's wishes without a word of grumbling or remonstrance; and on the following morning, when the other men started out, Ernest and Ralph set off on their way back to the station. There was no very well-defined track from the yards to Willaroo, but having done the journey several times before, they did not feel any doubt about finding their way. If they had kept straight along they would have arrived at the house early in the afternoon, but about noon they met with temptation in the shape of a kangaroo. Had it been only an ordinary one they would not have troubled about it, but it was *the* white one, and so was not to be passed by. They at once gave chase, and the kangaroo broke away at right angles to the course the boys had been taking. They soon got into country which was very rough and difficult to ride through, and being without a dog, there was nothing to be done but to run the animal until it was exhausted.

This took longer than they had expected, the rocky, scrub-covered ground hindering the movements of the horses. After about an hour's galloping, however, the kangaroo began to knock up, and at last stopped and faced its pursuers. Ernest jumped off his horse to get a stick, leaving his reins hanging on his horse's neck. Ralph did the same.

But now they found the kangaroo was not by any means so exhausted as they had thought. Upon their approach it turned tail and hopped away, but so slowly that the boys felt that they could soon run it down on foot. Excited by the chase, they thought nothing of time or distance, but followed the game through scrub and over rocky hills and waterless creeks. At last it disappeared round the shoulder of a hill, and when the boys, hot and panting, came to the spot, not a sign of the animal was to be seen. They hunted about and searched for some time longer, but all to no purpose. The mysterious white kangaroo had again eluded its pursuers!

"Well, it is singular!" exclaimed Ralph. "I made sure we had the brute this time. I don't wonder at the blacks thinking it is possessed of a 'Debil-Debil!'"

"It's most provoking!" assented Ernest, wiping his heated face. "But now let us get back to our horses.

What a lot of time we have wasted! The sun is quite low!"

But to find the horses was not so easy. They turned back in the direction in which they thought they had come, but nothing was to be seen of them.

"Either we have missed them," said Ernest at last, "or else they have run off home."

"Run away, I expect, Ern; I don't believe we left our reins hanging down, so there is nothing to stop them. I don't think it is much use trying to find them, they are certain to go home. What do you say if we make a bee-line across country, and not bother about the horses?"

"I am willing; but it will be late before we get to Willaroo."

CHAPTER XIV.

LOST.

OUR two boys trudged along, mile after mile, in almost total silence. They were vexed at the mischance that had befallen them through their stupidity, and they felt certain in their own minds that they could not reach Willaroo that night, and must necessarily pass it in the bush, and go without supper and also breakfast to-morrow morning. It is very easy to look upon this as being a not unpleasant adventure, when one is seated safely and comfortably in one's own home, midst friends and food, but Ralph and Ernest would have given a good deal to have found themselves seated in their saddles once more with the prospect of a hearty meal.

Their way led through tangled masses of scrub, low-lying hills, and sandy flats. In many places the undergrowth was so thick that they could not force their way through, but were obliged to go round about. They kept along the tops of the hills when possible, and looked eagerly around in search of some familiar landmark, but not one could they recognise; nothing met their view but miles of scrub stretching to the horizon on every side. The hills did not run in any particular direction, but seemed to be a confused jumble, while the gullies led one into another, and were useless to guide the boys in the direction to be taken.

Even a practised bushman would have been somewhat puzzled to find his way in this piece of country and would have been forced to put forth all his knowledge and experience to come out successfully in the end. And, of course, these lads, accustomed though they were to some extent to bush life, had never been put to so severe a test. Happily for them they did not know that they were bushed in a strip of country known as the "Never, Never" ranges. Their hearts would have sunk indeed, for by hearsay they had learned that it had got this ominous name on account of several persons having been lost in it, and never, never heard of again.

Now the boys are toiling up a hill from which, because it appeared to be higher than the others, they hoped to gain a better view. But disappointment awaited them! They stood side by side, and in front of them, behind them, and on both sides, they saw other hills equally as high. The sun was just dipping below the dark horizon of trees to the west, and in less than an hour's time darkness would be upon them.

"It's a pleasant look-out, Ern, old chap, isn't it?" said Ralph, feeling at the moment that his cousin had never been so much a companion as now.

"'Tis so!" answered Ernest, seating himself upon a lump of stone, and clasping his knees with his arms. "We shall not see Willaroo to-night, that's certain. The best thing we can do is to pick out a good camp and make the best of it, and pray that God will deliver us."

"I reckon we shall not have so pleasant a time of it as we had the last two nights. Will you feel in the mood for a song, Ernest, if I call upon you by-and-by?"

"Yes; an appropriate song would be "Far away!" Come on, it's no use sticking up here; the night will be cool enough presently without our rugs, and I suppose we shall have no fire."

"Oh, let me see! did I give that box of lucifers back to Brown, after lighting the fire at dinner-time yesterday? I hope I didn't! No, here they are. Hurrah! we'll not be so badly off after all; a fire will make things cheerful, anyway."

It was certainly a fortunate discovery, and the boys made their way down the hill in search of a sheltered camping-place, cheered in spirits at finding themselves better off than they had expected. They chose a spot of level ground at the foot of a clump of mallee; a number of trunks sprang from one root, and by breaking off boughs and weaving them through these, a very good breakwind was made. Of wood there was abundance, and in a short time Ralph had a fine fire blazing up, and sending forth showers of sparks. It wasn't needed for warmth, but it certainly did make things look more cheerful, and the boys' spirits rose in proportion.

"Now then, Ernest!" exclaimed Ralph, "be smart and get the supper laid out, and the tea ready to pop into the pots."

"Certainly, sir!" Ernest replied in the same spirit, but not moving an inch. He was lying at full length, his elbows on the ground, and his hands supporting his chin, and staring into the fire. "Will you have the lamb and mint sauce, or the cold turkey, to-night?"

"The turkey, by all means;' and I should prefer coffee to tea, for a change. But without joking, Ern, I am beginning to feel hungry, aren't you? and thirsty too. Our water-bags are on the saddles."

"I'm awfully thirsty," said Ernest with great fervour; "and I could eat the hardest chunk of salt meat that ever a fellow had, I believe — but I should want a drink first. I wonder if we can find any water?"

"I shouldn't wonder, the rain must have come out here. In fact, I saw some little holes of water in some rocks soon after we began to walk, but I wasn't thirsty then."

"Yes, I saw them too! Let's look about up this gully before it gets pitch dark."

They found a small supply not very far away, caught in a hollow of the bed of the watercourse; there was enough to give them each a drink and a drop to spare.

"If we only had the beef now!" exclaimed Ralph, wiping his mouth with his shirt sleeve. Their coats were fastened to the rugs on the horses.

"What do fellows eat when they are bushed in this way?" said Ernest. "We ought to be able to find something; how did people do in the books we have read so often?"

Ernest was almost saying "lost." The word was on the tip of his tongue, but he checked it in time.

"Oh, that was different, you know; they weren't really—er—" Ralph hesitated for a moment. "They weren't in our position really, you know; they were make-believes of the fellows who wrote the books, you know, whereas we are actually bushed for a time. It always surprised me what a wonderful lot of things those fellows used to find, just what they wanted, and just at the nick of time, too."

"Yes!" said Ernest; "and there was generally some wonderful fellow with them who knew everything, a kind of cyclopædia on two legs."

"I remember! a chap that dug away under one tree and fetched out ham and eggs, or something good to eat anyway; drove a gimlet—he always had a chest of tools with him — into another tree and tapped it for milk; and climbed another to gather nice hot rolls of bread-fruit. That's the fellow you mean!"

"That's the very man!" said Ernest, laughing. "What a jolly fellow you'd be if you could only do half as much!"

"Don't be too sure that I cannot," said Ralph. "But I tell you what, when we get back to Willaroo

I'll write to the papers and tell them just how we did get on. This scrub of ours isn't the pleasantest place when one's hungry."

"And we'll call it the 'Boys in the Bush.'"

"Or the 'Innocents in the Interior,'" added Ralph.

They amused themselves in this way for a little while, and then, feeling very hungry, but not liking to talk about it, they became silent. It is a very unpleasant thing when one has been in the habit of having three good meals every day to be suddenly cut off from them. The boys began to chew little pieces of stick, and this satisfied them in part; but it was nothing compared to two or three rounds from a home-made loaf of bread and plenty of meat and eggs and butter, such as the people at the station had before them, probably, at that very moment.

Suddenly, while they were picturing these things to themselves, a rustling of branches was heard, followed by a low snarl. Ralph sprang to his feet.

"Come here, Ernest," cried Ralph, looking about him for a stick; "I told you not to be too certain that I could not find food when necessary! What do you say to grilled 'possum?"

It was one of these animals they had heard in a tree close by. They searched about and soon found it, and Ralph, climbing a little way up the tree, knocked it down with his stick. Ernest rushed forward to seize it, but the 'possum was not dead, only stunned, and Ernest not being careful to take it by the tail received a sharp bite in his hand, which made him let go, and the 'possum scampered off and climbed another tree.

"Watch him, Ern! Don't let him escape!" shouted Ralph, slipping down the tree so quickly that he tore his trousers. "Follow him up, or we'll go supperless to bed! Do you see him?"

"Yes, all right! He's such a big one! I'll knock him off the tree and you look out below."

The 'possum had no chance this time, for the moment he touched he ground, Ralph hit it on the head with his stick and killed it. Then they took it down to the fire, skinned it, and cleaned it as well as they could; it didn't look very inviting certainly, being long and skinny and very much like a cat But you may be sure they were not inclined to be fastidious, and so, cutting it up with their pocket-knives, they laid pieces upon the fire to cook.

"It ought to be done now," said Ralph, when it had been cooking for about two minutes.

"It's no use being in a hurry," said Ernest. Then

they waited until the lumps of meat looked as black and charred as a piece of charcoal.

"What do you think of it?" asked Ralph presently, picking the last piece of meat off a leg.

"Not bad; though pretty strong of gum-leaves, isn't it?"

"I wouldn't mind that so much. It's the little bits of fur that bother me; one piece nearly choked me just now."

"It must have been an old 'possum, I fancy, the meat's so tough and stringy. But I say, it won't do to eat it all up, you know; we must leave some for breakfast."

"We had better hang it on a tree then, or the ants will be swarming over it in no time. It was lucky that 'possum made such a noise, or we would never have thought of looking for him. Let's put the skin along with the kangaroo's, it will be one more for our rug."

"It was something more than luck," said Ernest; "I believe that 'possum was *sent* to us, Ralph."

"I dare say it was, Ern; though one never thinks of those things somehow—at least I don't. We were very thankful for it anyway. though we didn't say so in words."

"Uncle says words are not always necessary as long as we feel sincerely and remember who sends us good things. Let's hang our meat up in the larder and then go to bed."

Both these matters were quickly accomplished. The remains of the 'possum were hung to an overhanging limb, and the boys, after throwing more wood upon the fire, stretched themselves side by side on the bare ground, said their prayers, and quickly fell asleep.

The sun was well up before Ralph awoke next morning. He must have been dreaming, because he called out, "Wake up, Ernest! There is the bell ringing." Ernest sat up at once, and then the boys remembered where they were. The fire had burnt very low, and they felt chilled, but quickly piled on fresh wood and warmed themselves. They found another little hole of water, and drank at it, and finished their 'possum for breakfast. Then they set out on their journey. They walked for many hours, but still they did not seem to be getting away from the hills and scrub. The country appeared to be of exactly the same character as that through which they had passed yesterday. Here and there they found water, but only in small rock holes. There were no springs or creeks, and if it had not been for the heavy thunderstorm on Sunday they would have discovered through how waterless a desert they were walking. While they walked they kept silence; one followed the other, and talking was not easy, and besides they were both becoming anxious and uncomfortable, and each feared to let the other see their uneasiness. Towards midday they rested a while, tired, hungry, and dispirited.

"We must surely be near some place we can recognise! We have been going in the right direction all along, don't you think?" It was Ernest who spoke.

"Yes, as far as I can tell, though I don't know very well where we are."

"At any rate the horses will go straight to the station, and will be seen by some of the people. Aunt will send some of the blacks back along the tracks with them, and they'll soon find us."

"I am afraid, Ern, that they will not go to the station. You see they have only just been brought in, and as sure as anything Pepper and your horse will make back to that part of the run where they have been running all along."

"Ah, perhaps they will! Then there is nothing for it but to keep tramping on until we come out somewhere. I hope that will be soon, because I'm getting tired, and feel jolly hungry too. I say, wouldn't it be grand to march into the house to-night and surprise them with the story of our being bushed? And what a stunning supper we'd have!"

"Ah, wouldn't we just! Well, come along; we shan't do it if we lie here all day. 'Tramp, boys, tramp, and be contented!'" Ralph tried to sing, but his throat was dry, and the words would not come.

On and on they went silently and with stubborn courage, but with surely failing strength. There was food within their reach, but they knew not of it; only a native could have shown them where to look. Gradually the sun sank lower and lower, the night was close at hand, but how far on towards home had they journeyed?

"Ralph!" said Ernest suddenly, "I think we shall soon come to some place we know; these hills seem familiar to me, do they to you? But I can't remember where I have seen them before. I wonder"——

Ernest's voice stopped suddenly. He had been following Ralph closely through a thick clump of scrub; they had got out on to a clear space, and there in front of them stood the breakwind—the camp—that they had that morning left!

CHAPTER XV.

CAPTURED BY BLACKS.

POOR lads! It was a terrible blow for them. During one whole day they had, as they thought, been nearing home at every step. And now they knew that they had been walking in a circle, that they were as far from Willaroo as ever, and that they were becoming weakened for want of proper food.

Ernest stared blankly before him, and then dropping upon the ground buried his face in his hands. Ralph's face turned deathly white. He placed his arm against the stem of a mallee and leant his forehead upon it. Taking his knife from his pocket, hardly knowing what he was doing, he began to cut and hack the bark from the tree. He felt that he must do something; the scrub and the hills, everything about him, appeared to be going round and round before his eyes. He was unable to think, hardly able for a time to realise, the position of his cousin and himself. After a few minutes, however, he aroused himself and stood up straight. He was the elder of the two, and upon him lay the duty of comforting and cheering his companion.

"Come, Ern, old chap! we've made a bad start, but don't be downhearted. Maybe we have been *brought* back to this place for an especial purpose. If we have been going the wrong way all day it was just as well to find it out at once. Come, man, rouse up! We must look about for a supper of some sort. We got a capital one here last night!"

Ernest sat up as Ralph spoke. There were traces of tears on his cheeks, but his cousin after one glance turned his eyes away from him

"We are lost! we are lost!" was all that the poor lad could say.

"Don't you believe it!" answered Ralph stoutly, forcing himself to appear more hopeful than he really was. "I believe I see the reason why we've come back, though I must say that I felt pretty queer just at first."

"What's the reason?" asked Ernest curiously.

"Why, don't you see, we can now track our steps back to where the horses left us, and "——

"Oh, yes, I see!" interrupted Ernest, rising to his feet and speaking cheerfully. "And then we can follow the horse-tracks "

"That's it! And if any one is tracking them from the station we shall soon meet them. That's why we've come back, I'm sure."

"I never thought of that," said Ernest quite briskly "But, Ralph, do you think we can track our steps back from here?"

"Oh, yes, I am certain we can; we've often seen the blacks tracking. You only want to keep your eyes wide open. But now the question is, Are we going to find another 'possum?"

"Oh, surely! I should say there's certain to be more than one 'possum about here. That fellow wasn't all alone, I'll be bound."

Cheered by the thought of the plan they had arranged for the next day, and which in fact was really the best they could have hit upon, the boys began their search for supper. They were certainly lucky fellows in some respects, for close to the tree where they had killed the first opossum they came upon a hollow log, and inside, in a cosy nest, were three others, one old one and two half grown. These were evidently, as Ernest suggested, "the other members of the family." That night they ate the two small ones, and very good they were, not being so strongly flavoured as the older one.

The boys did not sleep very soundly, they were anxious,

and also wanted to set out on their new route. Very early in the morning they were up, roasted a small piece of meat, and then prepared to start. The morning was perfectly calm, and the smoke from the camp fire went up towards the sky in a perfectly straight column of pale blue colour. It caught Ralph's eye.

"Look, Ernest, we could make some capital signals with smoke; it will save them a deal of trouble in tracking us. Don't you think it will be a good thing to light fires as we go?"

"Capital! Only we must be careful with the matches. We'll take a lighted stick along with us, and fire scrub here and there. If we throw green boughs on to the flames the smoke will be black and easier seen at a distance."

They were quite right, men *were* tracking them, and saw the smoke almost as soon as it was made.

The boys now began the work of retracing their steps, Ralph, as usual, taking the lead. But, oh, how different a thing was it in practice from what it had been in theory! Where the ground was soft and sandy they got on very well, but in the rocky ground, where they had gone up and down hill, the tracks were hardly to be seen, and in the scrub, where the undergrowth was thick, they could see nothing. And in this they were surprised to find how very little trace they had left, very few of the bushes being broken or disturbed. And another thing was that neither Ralph nor Ernest had ever before attempted to track.

Again and again Ralph lost the trail, and much time was lost in making casts to one side and the other in search of it. By midday they had covered a very little distance; so little, indeed, that they both became impatient, and resolved to proceed more boldly. For some time this answered very well, they would find traces here and there, then walk on and again fall in with them. This was satisfactory, because they knew now that they were going in the direction they wished to, and were not making another circle. At short distances apart Ernest would light up some dry brushwood and pile green boughs upon it, making smoke signals so frequently that any searchers would be able to tell the direction they were taking.

Hope still burned steadily within their breast, but they had much to contend with. The calm, still air, was admirable for smoke signals, but not so well suited for tramping through scrub and rock covered hills. They had not, so far, been distressed for lack of water, but could not help noticing how much smaller the supplies were becoming.

Slowly making their way through a belt of scrub, they were suddenly startled by the appearance of two natives. For an instant the boys fancied that they were friendly blacks, but they were soon undeceived. The blacks had heard them coming, and as Ralph came into sight one raised his spear as if about to hurl it at him.

It was an anxious moment for Ralph and Ernest. Retreat was out of the question; the natives were within thirty yards of them; there was no cover to hide behind, saving the bushes, and they would not afford protection against spears. There was nothing to be done but to look death, if death it was to be, bravely in the face. Resistance was hopeless. What chance had the boys unarmed against two natives well provided with spears, waddies, and boomerangs? None at all! Ralph saw this at a glance, and stood erect and motionless, waiting to receive the spear. It was possible that with the stick he carried he might be able to ward it off, and so preserve life for a few moments longer. Ernest stood beside him, equally composed. They saw the spear drawn back to give more force to its flight, and then, to their astonishment, the other black fellow raised his waddy and struck the weapon from the hand of his companion. At the same time he uttered some words in his own language, pointing towards the boys. Then both blacks came closer, and Ralph recognised in the man who had struck up the spear the very black that he and Ernest had rescued from hanging in the tree! They felt that their lives were saved. The reaction from despair to joy was too sudden, and they both fell unconscious to the ground.

If it be doubted that joy could so affect lads of the age of Ralph and Ernest, it must be borne in mind that their strength was reduced by the trials and privations they had endured. They soon came again to their senses, and when they sat up the natives grinned, nodded their heads, patted their chests, and in every possible way showed that they were pleased. But they showed this in a still more satisfactory way by placing food before the boys. This was in the shape of small loaves or cakes, and was made of seeds and other vegetable matter ground up and baked.

It was a strange-looking group that sat round the fire eating this primitive meal. The boys' clothes—or, more correctly speaking, rags—hung about them in tatters. The natives were not big men in any way, but strong and wiry-looking. Their skin appeared to be as thin as silk, and beneath it the working of every muscle could be seen at each movement they made. They were not, however, the noble-looking fellows that the natives are generally supposed to be. They had scanty whiskers and beards, rather thick lips, and their noses were almost level with their cheeks. The two front teeth of the upper jaw were missing, and this gave the men a very unpleasant expression.

And now the question occurred to the boys, Would these natives help them to get back to Willaroo, or would they keep them amongst their own tribe? The grilled 'possum and the cakes had made them feel very much better, and with renewed life came back the longing for home and friends.

"It's a rum look-out, isn't it?" said Ralph, when they had talked the question over a little.

"'Tis so! But uncle is certain to follow us up until he finds us, alive or dead Though we were such muffs at tracking, the Willaroo blacks will soon pick us up; it is not very likely that we shall have much rain at this time of year, and our trail will keep fresh for a long time."

"Well, if I've got any say in the matter. I hope we shall be found alive. I say, suppose we are kept here for years, and become white chiefs? I know some of the volunteer drill"

"Yes, and when we have learned their lingo we could teach them things we remembered out of books. Why, we might have schools for the young 'uns, and after a long time, when some explorers or other people came this way, they would find a civilised race of blacks."

"Maybe; we can't tell. But I don't know that I care about the idea, Ern. These blacks wouldn't be half such jolly fellows for chums as some of the boys at school are."

"Well, look here, you'd better try and make these fellows understand that we want to go home."

"I wonder what the beggars' names are? Can't you muster up any black fellows' talk, Ern? If you are going to be a missionary, this will be a jolly chance for you to learn the language, won't it? You'd better tackle them now."

Ernest rather demurred at this; but as Ralph insisted, and as he saw the men preparing to move, he gave in, and tried to explain what he wanted to their old acquaintance of the tree. "Willaroo! Willaroo!" he said, pointing first to Ralph and himself, and then in the direction in which he supposed the station lay. His friend understood, for he repeated the word, but pointed in quite a different direction to Ernest.

"He knows!" said Ralph; "he's a brick! Promise him some tobacco, Ern."

So the words "Willaroo" and "Bacca" were repeated again and again, and the native echoed them, but still pointed in the same direction as at first. They went on till sunset, and then formed a camp. Their supper was superior to that of the last two nights, for they had some native rats, and also some roots sweet to the taste, and a few more cakes. Without thought of fear, the boys slept soundly through the night.

CHAPTER XVI.

THE BLACK ENCAMPMENT.

EVIDENTLY, if the natives had any evil intentions towards the boys, they did not mean to put them at once into practice. For three days they travelled peacefully together, always finding water and food. That period gave the boys a lesson in bush lore that they are never likely to forget. From the ground the blacks dug up roots, which, when baked in the fire, were, though without much flavour, pleasant to eat; from the trunks of trees they extracted a large white grub,* twisting it out of its hole by the aid of a flexible twig, hooked at one end. These grubs were half as long as one's little finger, and of about the same thickness. The blacks popped them into their mouths just as they took them from the tree, and, judging from the way they smacked their lips, it was evident that they were a delicacy.

* This grub is allied to the English "Goat moth."

Ralph and Ernest fought shy of them for a while, though offered to them by the natives; but hunger and curiosity combined to conquer the objection to put a big wriggling grub into their mouths, and on the second day Ralph, shutting his eyes, popped one in and closed his teeth upon it. Ernest watched his face for signs of disgust, but no such thing was to be observed; on the contrary, Ralph opened his eyes very wide and exclaimed, "Why, they're real good, Ern! They've got a nice nutty flavour. You try this fellow," handing one to him as he spoke.

Ernest swallowed it without shutting his eyes, and from that moment both he and Ralph provided themselves with hooked twigs, and rivalled the blacks in the eagerness of their search for this peculiar food. There were other grubs to be found in the ground, and these were unearthed either by means of a wooden instrument shaped like a gouge, or by the aid of the hooked twig. But the great thing with the blacks was nardoo. This is a plant which sends up slender stems several inches high; at the tip is a flower-like leaf divided into four nearly equal parts. It bears a fruit or seed, and this is the part used for food. It is pounded into meal between two stones, and is made up in the form of cakes and baked in the ashes. It is said to be nourishing when eaten with animal food, but taken alone to afford no support.

Up to the third day the boys had travelled under the belief that they were being guided towards Willaroo. Then they began to wonder why they were not coming upon familiar country. Calculating first the distance they had hunted the white kangaroo, and then the miles they had walked in a circle on the second day, they felt sure that they could not have been very far distant from the station, or, at any rate, from those parts of the run which were known to them. And now, during these three days they must have walked at least sixty or seventy miles, and still there were no landmarks they could recognise. At Ralph's suggestion Ernest repeated the words "Willaroo" and "Bacca;" and, as before, the natives echoed the words and pointed in the way they were going.

"I believe those fellows are a couple of humbugs," said Ralph, after they had proceeded a little farther. "Let us stop and show them that we are determined to go our own way."

"But suppose we go wrong again? we shall be as badly off as before! Why should they want to mislead us?"

"That's only known to themselves. But I'm con-

"Then came the sudden meeting, the spear poised to throw, and in fact the whole scene reacted."—*See Page* 127.

vinced we are not going right. We could get on quite well by ourselves, now that we know how to find food. Just let us try the effect of a mutiny."

They did so, and just as so many mutineers before them have done they discovered that authority in arms is not to be resisted with impunity. At first the natives only grinned, and tried to persuade the boys by beckoning them on, and repeating "Willaroo," but when they saw this to be of no avail, and that the lads were determined to go their own way, their manner changed. They raised their spears and stood in front of them, barring the way.

"It's no use!" said Ralph; "they are our masters, and we must obey. But I am sure now that we are going into their own country."

"I am afraid so, too!" answered Ernest. "Only there's nothing for it but to go; we may manage to escape some time, perhaps, or be rescued by Uncle and the men. Come on, it is no use; we shall only be waddied."

So, the boys had to go unwillingly, in the direction pointed out to them, and they noticed that the natives watched them very closely, and when travelling kept rather behind them.

On the evening of the fourth day their suspicions

were verified. They had made an unusually long march, and towards evening entered country that was very much superior in its appearance to that through which they had passed. The rocky hills gave way to plains, the trees and scrub were of finer growth and grew in clumps, between which lay well-grassed flats. Kangaroos became more numerous; birds, which hitherto had been wanting, could now be seen, wheeling in flocks above the trees; a spring of water was passed bubbling out from beneath a huge rock; and once, at a great distance off, the men had pointed to a number of emus running through the bushes. The presence of birds was a sufficient sign that the country was well watered, and that it grew grass and berry-bearing bushes, for in deserts where water is not permanent they are never to be found.

The natives now walked steadily forward, paying no heed to the game to be seen on every side of them. They made towards a wooded hill, and as they approached the boys could see numerous wreaths of smoke curling upward against the dark background.

A short time after sunset they arrived at a large encampment of natives; a countless pack of dogs rushed out, barking furiously; and amid shouts of welcome the two natives, with Ralph and Ernest between them, became the centre of a group of excited savages. The jabbering of tongues was deafening, and the boys had to submit to a very close examination. Their captors had treated them wonderfully well, not having, for one thing, shown any surprise at their clothing or their white skins. But now, after staring at the lads, several men and children pressed upon them with exclamations of surprise. Ralph saw his hat passed from one to another, each man trying it upon his head; the children imitated the men, until one picaninny, having buried his head in it, and not being able to pull it off, began to roar with fear: he was at once released, and the hat returned to Ralph. The same thing was being endured by Ernest, but, unfortunately, his hat reached the outer circle of women, and when Ernest last saw it, it was being pulled to pieces in a fight between two of them. Their shirts and trousers being evidently taken as a kind of a loose skin, excited great surprise, until the friendly black—who appeared to have assumed the part of showman—opened Ralph's shirt and showed his white skin. This sight was greeted by exclamations of wonderment, and a score of dirty black fingers kept touching and pinching it until Ralph began to fear they would make a hole in his chest.

'I do hope,' he said to Ernest—and as he spoke the

crowd stopped jabbering to listen—"I do hope that these people have no scientific man amongst them, or a museum in want of specimens, or we shall surely be stuffed and labelled."

The curiosity of the natives was satisfied for the moment, and their hospitable customs came into play. The boys and their two black companions were liberally supplied with nardoo cakes, roast rats, and other dainties, washed down with water from a neighbouring spring. While they feasted—and our boys took their full share of everything—the members of the tribe squatted around them and kept up an incessant talking. The captives could not understand a word, but supposed their friends were being closely questioned on the incidents that had befallen them in foreign parts. The talk lasted beyond the time occupied in eating, and Ralph and Ernest lay resting on their elbows, watching with interest the swarms of picaninnies and dogs that moved constantly round, and over and in between the men, fighting, snarling, and chattering without intermission, and unheeded by their seniors and masters. But by-and-by a movement was made amongst the men. A few came forward strangely decorated, and the boys knew that a corroberie * was about to be given.

* A song and dance performance.

CHAPTER XVII.

LIFE WITH THE BLACKS.

THE natives' camp was on the edge of an open flat at the foot of a hill. The scrub in the background formed a shelter from the wind and provided wood for the fires, and the flat was an admirable place upon which to practise spear and waddy throwing. The wurleys in which the different families slept were nothing more than a rude shelter made of boughs of trees fixed in the form of a half circle, and a stick supporting the roof in the middle. It might be compared to a large umbrella cut in two. These wurleys were dotted about without any attempt at order or method, and a small fire burnt in front of each. There were quite two hundred blacks, without counting the children, and a wurley was occupied sometimes by a large family of ten or a dozen.

Ralph and Ernest were interested in everything that was going on, notwithstanding the anxious position in which they found themselves. It was nothing that they had been kindly welcomed and fed—the natives would be equally as kind to their greatest foe, and murder him the next moment. But they see no harm in this—'tis the custom of the tribe; and as liars they stand pre-eminent. They not only lie to white men, but to each other.

And yet, notwithstanding these vices, they are hospitable, and they reverence old age, and love their children as much as their dogs. That means a great deal. Beat a black fellow's child and he is offended with you; strike his dog and he will fly into a terrible passion. The dogs are of great assistance in hunting; and if one gets wounded or killed the lamentation over it is great.

But now the blacks were preparing for the corroberie, and the boys were determined to see all that was worth seeing. They had seen corroberies at Willaroo amongst the tame blacks, but there the performers were few. This one was evidently to be on a large scale.

The corroberie was at one time supposed by the whites to be a religious ceremony, but this is not the case. It is simply a rude dramatic representation of incidents in the everyday life of the tribe, such as hunts and fights; or it sometimes happens that the leader of the dance describes scenes that neither he nor any of his listeners have ever seen or experienced. The song is a monotonous chant in which the events are described, and consists of from one to three verses, and these are repeated over and over again. The chief feature in the dance is the wonderfully accurate time that is kept. On this evening sixty men appear, decorated to the utmost extent that their means will allow. There is no moon, but a double line of fires is lighted, and made to flare with dry leaves and brushwood, and between these the dance takes place.

For the time Ralph and Ernest have ceased to think of their home and friends—they squat beside the fires and help the blacks to keep them flaming; the flickering light falls upon scores of black faces, shining eyes, and white teeth. The performers range themselves in single file at one end of the ground. A number of old men and about twenty women form the orchestra; the men beat two sticks together something after the manner of bones in a Christy Minstrel performance, and the women strike with their hands upon dried skins tightly folded up into a pad. The piece to be acted is the arrival and welcome of the two natives and the white boys. Two men and two lads of about the same age as our boys stand at the end of the ground opposite the others. The music begins, the rattle of the sticks and the drumming of the skins blending strangely with the chant sung by the old men. At first it is very low,

Then the travellers advance, keeping time to the music by bringing the right foot smartly down upon the ground, and striking their other leg with the left hand they advance a little way and halt, still beating time. Now the first sixty men come on, and the earth seems to tremble as their feet come down together. The four travellers now move on again, and as the two parties come near to one another the music increases in sound and the time becomes quickened. But before they quite meet the travellers turn back; they are making a journey. The music dies away as the travellers go back, then becomes louder as they return. The end comes with a sort of triumphal march up and down, the dancers excite themselves until they foam at the mouth, and the chant grows more wild.

In a moment, at the height of passion, a signal is given by the leader, and the whole thing suddenly ceases. The performers retire, and the onlookers shout their approval. This has been done in honour of the returned men; they were influential persons in the tribe, and in this way their standing was recognised.

But as yet there was no movement made to break up the assembly. Natives are as much given to the keeping of late hours for amusements as are their white brothers and sisters. A cry ran from mouth to mouth,

"They overtook the men at the end of a long day's ride, and at first it appeared as if a fight

and the names of the travellers were called again and again. The one that had befriended the boys appeared first, and the blacks welcomed him by the name "Apirrie!* Apirrie!" Then the second followed and was addressed as 'Thidnara!"† They were both decorated with chalk marks and boughs, and carried spears and waddies. As the music began the boys saw that these fellows were about to show how they captured the whites. The two native lads representing Ralph and Ernest advanced from the opposite end in a slow, dazed, hesitating way, and the men pretended to be tracking and searching bushes and behind rocks. Then came the sudden meeting, the spear poised to throw, and in fact the whole scene reacted. It was true to life, and Ralph and Ernest shouted " Bravo!" and "Encore!" as the men retired.

The natives did not leave off their songs and dances until a very late hour. Then Ralph and his cousin were taken to Apirrie's wurley and were given a couple of skin rugs for a bed. The other occupants were the man, a woman, four children, and six dogs. The dogs nestled close up to the edges of the rugs; one, indeed, who appeared to be a special favourite, scratched his way underneath and slept peacefully in

* Father † Nephew

the arms of one of the children. For some time the boys talked together, trying to devise means of escape. But they were both very tired, and soon fell asleep.

It was late in the morning before the camp was astir, and the day was passed very idly. The men had been out hunting the day before, and had plenty of food in store. The women went out to dig roots and grubs and to gather nardoo, and then busied themselves in baking and grinding it into meal. The open flat was the scene of the greatest activity. Here the young members of the tribe, from the picaninny that could barely toddle up to boys of fourteen or fifteen years of age, practised throwing spears, waddies, and boomerangs. The white boys looked on, rather envying the dexterity shown in spear-throwing; they were tired of doing nothing, and longed to join the others.

By signs Ralph made Apirrie understand that he wished to join in the boys' sport, and was given some weapons from the wurley. Though the spears were much lighter than those used by the men, Ralph and Ernest found that they were quite heavy enough for an unpractised thrower.

The tribe had no fixed hours for meals, the natives eating whenever they felt hungry, and, as a rule, they either had a feast or a famine. The boys found that Apirrie's lubra was an excellent cook. She did most of the work, looked after the picaninnies, and scolded her husband. During the day Apirrie knocked over some birds, and gave orders to have two of them cooked at once. With her digging-stick the lubra made a hole in the ground, placed a stone at the bottom, and filled it with fire. While this was burning and heating the hole, she took the birds to the spring, and, mixing up mud, coated them thickly with it, just as they were, feathers and all. The birds were transformed into two shapeless lumps of clay. When the hole was sufficiently hot the birds were put in, live embers packed all round, and upon the top a covering of green boughs to keep the steam in. When they were supposed to be cooked, Apirrie was called, and the birds taken out. The clay envelope was broken open, and with it came away all the feathers, leaving the flesh ready to be eaten and full of natural juice. Apirrie took one bird, and gave the other to Ralph and Ernest. They thought that nothing had ever tasted so good!

But warlike exercises and high-art cooking were not the only things to be seen in a black's camp. During the day two of the men had a quarrel, and after yelling at each other for some minutes their friends interfered and proposed a duel, just in a friendly way, to show that there was no ill-feeling on either side. The men agreed to this, and walked off to their wurleys to select waddies. Then they came out on to the flat, several men and Ralph and Ernest standing by as witnesses. The duellists approached one another, and one hurled his waddy upon the ground; it sprang up, hitting the other man a fearful blow on the head.

"That was a good one!" said Ralph. "What thick heads these fellows must have!"

"They must so!" answered Ernest; "a blow like that would have killed a white man. Look at what they are doing now! I wish we could understand their lingo!"

The native who had received the blow had not attempted to avoid it; it was simply a challenge, and not worthy of further notice. Then he held his head down, and his antagonist, picking up his waddy, walked up to him. Coming within striking distance he laid the waddy upon the man's head for a moment, so as to take aim, and then raising it brought it down as hard as he could hit. It stunned him, and the duel was at an end.

CHAPTER XVIII.

THE NATIVES PREPARE FOR A JOURNEY

FOUR days passed away, and Ralph and Ernest were getting heartily tired of living amongst the natives, and longed for home. Even school was far preferable to this. Not so very long ago, both these lads had had a desire to go with the natives; they used to talk about it at school, and think what a pleasant life it must be—nothing to do but hunt all day long and sleep in the open air at night, now and then, perhaps, to go with the tribe to punish some other natives who had been guilty of wrong. They knew that the blacks about the stations were not a very high-minded people, but then they thought that this might be due to the evil influence of bad white men, and that they would find the wild blacks very different people. But, alas! how different had experience shown them to be! They had good qualities, it was true, but even the short time during which the boys had been with them was sufficient to show how very degraded a nation they were.

On several occasions they went out hunting with the men. During one of these orgies the boys tried to escape, but found that, though they were left unmolested in camp, they were yet strictly watched. Two men caught them up before they had gone many miles and forced them to return. After that a stricter watch was set, and they were not taken out to the next hunt, but left under the guard of two of the men. This failure disheartened the lads terribly—they began to fear they were prisoners for life, that their friends were not searching for them, or had given them up for lost.

"O Ralph," said Ernest, his voice trembling, "shall we never get away, do you think? I would rather have died out in the scrub than live here amongst these wretched people."

"So say I, lad!" Ralph had answered. "But I don't see how we are going to manage it just yet. It's a difficulty to get away from Apirrie's wurley at night, or we might have tried that game."

"Even then the natives would overtake us next day."

"They very likely would, and kill us, too! I don't want to make our friend angry if I can help it. It strikes me that he has saved our lives once or twice since we have been here"

"Yes, I am sure he has. Only the other day, that

scowling fellow in the next wurley would have speared us with pleasure, I am certain, just because I upset one of his dirty picaninnies. Then Apirrie picked up his waddy and spears and explained matters for our benefit."

"I like old Apurie. I'd take him out of a tree again to-morrow if I found him hanging there. Well, look here, the only thing we can do is to chum in—or pretend to, any way—with these people, and throw them off their guard, and then make another try for liberty"

Next morning the boys saw that the natives were going to shift camp. They never remained at a place where a death had occurred, as in the case of the black boy, and very seldom ever again revisited it. The direction taken by them was south, and Ralph and Ernest hoped they would travel down so near to the settlements of the whites as to make their chances of escape easier. They had begun to fear that no rescue party was on their track, and that if they were to get away from the blacks at all, it must be by their own unaided exertions. On one or two nights lately they had left their wurley in order to test their chance of sneaking away, but on each occasion the dogs had heard them, and had barked furiously Natives had poked out their heads and watched the movements of the lads until they returned to their wurley down at heart and disappointed at finding how difficult would be the execution of their plan. They had no idea of the direction of Willaroo; and this move of camp might, or might not, be to their advantage The tribe travelled for two days, making only temporary shelters at night, but on the second they unpacked their belongings, and the boys guessed that this camp was to be a more permanent one.

The wurleys were carefully built, ovens dug out, and a supply of roots and meat brought in. Ralph and Ernest built their wurley at the outside edge of the camp, in what they considered a position particularly favourable to stealing away at night. But to their disgust, and also alarm, one of the men placed his wurley in such a position and so close as to form a perfect guard. Ralph tried to get him to move, but the man only grinned and shook his head. It was evident that the natives guessed their intentions. But why they should object to let them go away the boys could not imagine. They were not useful to them in any way, and if the intention was to kill, and perhaps eat them, why wasn't it done at once? Neither of the boys had gained flesh, notwithstanding the hearty meals they ate of rats and kangaroo, lizards, roots, and nardoo; and as Ralph remarked, if the blacks didn't kill them soon they would be too thin to be worth bothering about.

On the day following their arrival at this camp the natives began to dig a hole about five hundred yards distant. When finished it was two feet deep, twelve feet long, and about ten wide.

"This looks uncommonly like a large oven," said Ernest to Ralph, as they sat beneath the shade of a tree looking on. "I wonder if they intend to bake us in it when finished?"

"But it is too big!" replied Ralph

"Oh, but perhaps they are going to catch an enemy or two, and make a jolly good feast."

"Well, they *might*, of course, only I don't see why they want to make the oven so long beforehand. First catch your enemy, you know, just the same as first catch your hare."

CHAPTER XIX.

PLANS OF ESCAPE.

THE month had been very dry—the ground was hard and bare of vegetation. The grass had been burnt up by the sun and swept away by the hot north winds. The springs of water were running low—animals of all kinds were moving away to other countries, and became scarcer every day. The women grumbled at the hardness of the ground—it was difficult to get the roots out; and luxuries in the way of grubs had disappeared altogether. The tribe could not very well follow the game on account of infringing the rights of other tribes. If they trespassed on their hunting-grounds war would be the result. In short, they wanted rain, the one thing needful to make the country in the interior a paradise both for blacks and whites, and this hole in the ground was the initial work in the process of making rain.

For the next day or two nothing of any consequence

occurred—the men did a little hunting, but had no very great success. The life was intolerably dull, and had it not been that our boys had attained a wonderful faculty for sleeping at all sorts of hours, the time would have hung most heavily upon their hands. One evening, however, they began to suspect that the natives had something important on hand; they gathered into little groups apart from the wurleys, and talked in low tones. If any of the lubras came near, the talking ceased until she had passed. On the very next morning at sunrise the boys were awakened by a fearful noise of shrieking, yelling, hooting, and hissing. Leaving their wurley they saw all the men, the old ones leading, marching away from the camp fully armed and decorated, and singing one of their weird, melancholy chants. The screaming and hooting arose from the women, and was intended to induce their husbands to stay at home! A little distance from the camp the men halted and talked amongst themselves

"I wonder what they are up to?" said Ernest.

"Off on some expedition or other, I should say, from the look of them. They've got all their weapons and travelling-gear as well."

"What shall we do—stay here or go with them?"

"I don't see any use in going with them. We don't

know where they are going, or what they are going for. Perhaps to fight with some tribe."

"I should rather like to see a fight."

"I wouldn't mind; but I don't care to be knocked on the head just to indulge my curiosity."

"No! that would be making the bump of curiosity too much of a good thing altogether!"

"Besides, by staying in one place we make it easier for any people who are looking for us to catch up. If the men are going away for any time we shall have a good chance of sneaking off. They evidently don't intend that we should go with them."

"And they don't intend to leave us quite to our own free-will either. Look! Here are all the old men returning, and the others are going on See how they turn back and wave their hands. They must be going on a long journey.* What a horrible row those lubras kick up!"

"Never mind, let's see after breakfast. I saw some fairly fat rats brought in last night. I hope the old woman will give us a good share of them, and not

* The men were starting upon a journey of several hundred miles in search of red ochre, used by them very largely They would be away from six to eight weeks The women fear that they may be killed on the way by hostile blacks. Each man will return carrying a cake of ochre of seventy pounds' weight on his head They travel twenty miles a day.

let those picaninnies eat most of them as she usually does."

Ralph was lucky in the matter of rats for breakfast. The "old woman," as he irreverently termed Apirrie's lubra, had not given most of them to the picaninnies, and both he and Ernest made a particularly good meal.

During the next few days they witnessed preparations made by the old men according to instructions given them by those who had gone on the expedition for red ochre.

Every morning the women were sent away from the camp, and were not permitted to return until sunset. But they were not allowed to be idle; seeds and roots had to be gathered and stored for a future home-coming feast, and from the dryness of the season the work was very hard.

The old men also worked, and in some matters allowed the boys to help them. The first thing to be done was to pull down most of the old wurleys and put up others. These new ones were built with a great deal of care, and in many ways were superior to the ordinary ones. They were for the use of the men when they returned, and were not to be inhabited until that time. When the very last touches had been given, a space, measuring about one hundred yards, was cleared and swept all round them. Bushes, stones, sticks, everything was taken away, and the ground left as bare and as clean as a courtyard. Why these special huts are built, or why such pains are taken in sweeping and garnishing, I do not know, nor have I been able to discover from those intimate with native habits and customs.

Ralph and Ernest had found the life dull, even when the whole tribe were together and hunting excursions frequent, but it became trebly so when nobody remained at the camp but the old men and the women and children. The men did not even care to bother about hunting, but lived on roots and lizards, and anything else that could be obtained without great exertion. The only thing that seemed to be of advantage to them in this quiet time was that it offered a better chance of escape. Still, the old men were a great obstacle, and they occupied wurleys placed near to that of the two boys. The attempt must be made, however, sooner or later, and they determined to try on the first pitch-dark night that came. If they were followed, they must try to make a fight for liberty. It would, they thought, be almost better to die in the attempt than to live as they were. They had now been amongst the natives for some weeks, and if any one was in search of them they surely would have appeared before now.

A day came at last which promised to give them the dark night they required. In the afternoon the clouds overspread the heavens in thick masses, there was hardly any wind, and the chances were that they would remain through the night. The hearts of the boys beat high with feelings of hope. Would they be successful? and would the night ever come?

The tediousness of waiting, however, was broken by a curious little incident. One of the picaninnies while running fell and sprained one of its wrists, and of course began to howl as loudly as it could. The mother rushed and picked it up, and, after the manner of all mothers, no matter what their colour may be, tried to pacify it, but to no purpose. Then the boys saw a custom practised which is supposed to relieve the injured child of its pain. The mother, aunts, cousins, and other relations of still more remote degree, bent down their heads and received blows from a boomerang until the blood trickled down over their foreheads. The same custom is observed in cases where a native has done any awkward thing, and thereby caused the others to laugh. He or she, as the case may be, asks one of the others to strike her on the head, and as soon as the blood flows she begins to laugh and pretends to enjoy the joke.

CHAPTER XX.

A PITCH DARK NIGHT.

THE sun went down at last, though they thought the afternoon had been the longest they had ever experienced. Supper was eaten, and in the course of an hour or two the natives rolled themselves in their rugs and went to sleep. The boys followed their example in everything but sleeping. They lay awake side by side, now and then speaking to each other in the softest of whispers. Fires, as usual, burnt before the entrance to every wurley, and by-and-by they sank low and their light became dim. Now was the best time to creep away. Slowly, and with the utmost caution, Ralph and Ernest slipped from beneath their rugs. They arranged them so that in the morning, if any of the natives looked in, they might suppose that the boys were still beneath them.

But now came the worst part of the affair—to get past the wurleys unnoticed by dogs or men. Ralph went first. Lying down upon his face he began to crawl along the ground, and Ernest followed closely enough to be able to just touch his cousin's feet. The night was intensely dark—no better one could have been chosen; but it was necessary that the boys should keep together. If once they became separated it would be very difficult to meet again, and neither of them would have left his companion behind on any consideration.

It was slow work, indeed! Ralph as he put out each hand had to feel that there were no stones, sticks, or bushes in his path; then he would gently draw his body along, using great care not to make the slightest noise. Two wurleys had to be passed. The fires were smouldering, and the dogs could be seen lying about them. It was possible to keep just outside the circle of light, and this the boys did; but as they were immediately in front of the first wurley, a stick beneath Ernest's knees snapped. Two of the dogs raised their heads, but did not bark. The boys lay quite still, hardly daring to breathe; several minutes passed which, to them, seemed as long as so many hours. Then the dogs got up, turned themselves round, lay down again, and apparently went to sleep. Ralph still did not move—he was trembling with excitement; at last Ernest touched his foot as a signal to go on, and then the crawling recommenced. They neared the second wurley,

Slowly, oh, so slowly! they crept along. They were now almost past it, when, right in the path they had to take, Ralph saw a dog crouching down gnawing a bone. Its head was from them, and they were not seen; but what was to be done? On one side was the wurley, and on the other a mass of bushes through which they could not pass without making a noise. Again our boys had to stop; but Ernest, not being able to see what was the cause, kept signalling Ralph to go on. Finding that this was unheeded, he crept up alongside, and then saw the dog. The poor lad's heart failed him: here was an obstacle indeed! The dog might see them and begin to bark at any moment

That moment came. The dog left gnawing the bone, and raised its head—it had probably scented the boys. They gazed at it almost fascinated with nervous fear. Sniffing the air, the dog turned round and caught sight of them; it was within a distance of six feet. A low growl came—the boys shivered; the dog came a little closer, looking at them fixedly. Then to their joy it wagged its tail—it had recognised them! It was one of Apirrie's dogs, and had made especial friends with Ralph, usually choosing his rug to lie upon at night. It came up to them, and the boys patted it. It was a mangy, hairless brute, but it was friendly, and either of the boys would have hugged it merely for that reason. They felt that there was now little danger to fear from its barking, and began to crawl on as before. When the dog came to its bone it took it up and walked away, and soon the boys were past the light and shrouded in the darkness.

CHAPTER XXI.

A SEARCH PARTY.

I MUST now leave the boys for a little while, slowly crawling along the ground, and return to Willaroo.

It is to be hoped that my readers may remember that, after the horses galloped away, the boys debated the point whether they would make back straight to the station, or would stay upon some favourite feeding-ground. The latter course was the one they pursued.

When Saturday night came, Mrs. Everdale watched for her son and nephew; but as the evening passed and they did not come, she concluded that they were staying for a day or two longer cattle-mustering. Sunday and Monday came and went, and Mrs. Everdale wondered at their absence, and felt a little hurt and lonely because they were not with her. She only had her son for a few weeks every year, and very naturally wished to see as much of him as possible. Then the day came when it was just a week from the time the musterers rode away, and still no boys. Mrs. Everdale began to get anxious, but comforted herself with the reflection that they were with Mr. Everdale, and very probably enjoying themselves exceedingly. And why should she grudge them the pleasure? she asked herself. Cattle-hunting was far pleasanter for them than spending their time about the house, with no one to talk to but herself. Still she could not help speaking of it to Smith, when next she went down to visit him.

"Come home!" he exclaimed, as though surprised at so sensible a woman as Mrs. Everdale thinking of such a thing. "No, no, ma'am, don't you believe it! If them boys turn up here before the other chaps, my name ain't Smith, that's all! Why, it ain't in reason! Here are two young chaps fresh from school; they gets their horses and they goes a musterin'; musterin's better than hunting, and they knows it as well as you or me, ma'am. I'd bet my last sixpence that at this here very moment they are a-tearing through the scrub as hard as they can go after some bullock—or maybe it's a cow, which are more contrary like—and using their new whips on the beast's hide. Don't you be afeard, ma'am—they're as right as ninepence. Boys is boys, and we'd do the same ourselves, ma'am—least, beg yer pardon. I would of I was them.

There was a good deal of truth in what Smith said, and Mrs. Everdale felt less anxious, but longed for the boys to return nevertheless. In the evening, while she was sitting reading in the drawing-room, Sambo poked his head in at the door and said, "I say, missis!"

"What is it, Sambo?"

"What name horse Ralph ride long a-cattle?"

"Pepper. Why do you ask?"

"Oh! What name Ernest ride?"

"Guerilda. But what do you mean?"

"Um! Pepp'r an' G'rilda, berry good. I say, G'rilda all same like it flour-bag?* an' Pepp'r all a-same like it, flour-bag an'—an'—an'—curr'nts?" †

"Yes; but do say what you mean, Sambo! Why do you talk like that?"

"Oh, me see um those horses to-day! got um saddles, got um bridles, no got um Ralph, no got um Ernest; saddle all along here"—Sambo patted his waistcoat—"no along back; me think um boys tumble down long a-scrub. S'pose you give um 'bacca, missis, me find um?"

Poor Mrs. Everdale was terribly frightened. The boys had no doubt been on their way home, and had been thrown; perhaps at this moment they were lying

* White colour   † White and black spots

out on the run, either dead, or, worse still almost, with some of their limbs broken and unable to move. These and other horrible thoughts rushed through her mind. What could she do? Send for Mr. Everdale? Send out to look for the boys? She questioned Sambo more closely to see if he were simply telling untruths for the sake of tobacco. But he held to his original version. At this moment a step came along the verandah, and Smith came to the door. He was well enough now to walk slowly about the place

"O Master Sambo! you're here already, are you! I reckon'd as much. I s'pose, ma'am, he's been telling you a yarn about them horses?"

"Yes! and I am dreadfully frightened about it. Some accident must have happened to the boys. What shall I do?"

"Don't you be frightened, Mrs. Everdale! I guess I know how it is. That Pepper is a regular nut to hook it if you let him go anywhere. Very likely the boys have got off to have a drink, or light a fire or somethin', and been careless like, and the horses have took to their heels. I expect they are back in camp now. They're no great distance away from where the musterers are, I feel sure."

"Do you really think that is likely, Smith?"

"I do, ma'am! I'd bet my last sixpence on it this moment. In the morning Sambo might ride out and see about them, or I might go, for that matter."

"No, certainly not! Mr. Everdale said you were not to get on a horse for some time yet. Send Sambo. But I do hope you're right in what you think!"

"Pretty sure of it, ma'am! Good night. Come along, Sambo; don't you stand idling about here all night."

As Smith spoke he walked Sambo off. But when he got away from the house, he said, "Sambo, you like um 'bacca?"

"My word, berry good, Mr. Smith!"

"Plenty long a store. Now suppose you catch a horse for me quick in this paddock, me give 'bacca to-night when Mr. Everdale come home; you see?"

The bribe was sufficient. Sambo went off at once, and by some means or other managed to catch a horse. Then Smith saddled it, and with difficulty and some pain mounted. He went slowly until he was well away from the house. Then he stopped for a moment, tightened his girths without dismounting, and murmuring to himself, "There's a mess somewhere; them boys is dead or lost," struck his horse with the spur, and through the night rode the forty miles to where Mr. Everdale was camped. He arrived there at dawn, faint and weary, just as the men were preparing to ride out.

The work amongst the cattle was at once stopped. Two of the men were sent off to bring in Pepper and Guerilda to the camp, and Mr. Everdale rode home to comfort his wife, and to prepare for the search of the missing boys. He stayed at Willaroo only for a few hours, and then returned to the stockman's camp accompanied by Sambo as tracker. The quickest method of finding them was to try and follow their tracks from the point where they were last seen. The two horses had been found and brought in; the saddles were complete, and there were no signs of the boys having been dragged by the stirrup.

At the first streak of light on the following morning the camp was astir. The searchers consisted of Mr. Everdale, Sambo, and Smith, who would go in spite of his master's remonstrances to the contrary. Of the other men, one returned to the station to remain and receive any news that might come in from other quarters, and two others were despatched to neighbouring sheep stations to inquire if the boys had been seen there.

But the tracking was the main thing to be depended upon, and Sambo became an important personage from the fact that he, in common with most blacks, possessed the faculty of running a trail that, to the eye of a European, was invisible. Smith was very good at this also, having been much amongst the natives, but was nevertheless much inferior to Sambo. The footmarks left by the boys' horses were easily followed. Sambo pointed out where they had turned aside, and also that they had been galloping.

"Those fellers run berry quick along here," he said; 'berry likely um try catch um kangaroo. Yes! you see? track down there where um claw go on ground, an' where um tail come along. Him run berry fast here."

Until they came to the place where the boys had jumped off their horses, the trail was so plain that Sambo could follow it from his saddle, but here he pulled up and dismounted.

After looking about, and ordering Mr. Everdale and Smith to remain where they were, so as not to confuse the marks, he came back to them and said, "Boys gone this way 'long a-foot, horses gone that a-way very quick; boys follow kangaroo, think um catch um by'm-by."

The real state of the case was easily to be understood, and leaving the horse-tracks, Sambo was told to keep to that of the boys. This was more difficult; the ground was stony and hard, and the white men could see nothing. Sambo was now on foot, and here and there he would point in silence to a stone misplaced, a broken twig, or a shred of cloth hanging to a bush, torn from the clothes of Ralph or Ernest.

CHAPTER XXII.

TRACKING.

Amongst the rocky hills through which the boys had followed the kangaroo the trail was constantly lost, and Sambo would require time to pick it up again. This he usually effected by casting about in a circle, or sometimes going back on the trail and running it afresh. These delays chafed the patience of Mr. Everdale and Smith. But they had to bear it—nothing else could be done. To travel aimlessly about the country would be useless, for if the boys were lying anywhere injured the searchers might pass within ten yards of them and be none the wiser. Neither of the white men had suggested that the boys might be dead, though such a thing was quite possible, but they kept eager watch for sudden risings of flights of carrion crows, or eagle hawks perched upon trees.

Nobody, except one who has taken part in a search for lost men in the bush, can imagine the ghastly interest attaching to these birds of prey as they wheel overhead or suddenly shoot down into the scrub wherever a carcase may happen to be.

The searchers reached the first camp made by the boys a little while before sunset, and stayed there for the night. Mr. Everdale had noticed that Sambo appeared puzzled as they came near to this place, but on being questioned he said that he had still got the trail, and everything was all right. But, in fact, the back tracks of the boys had been noticed by Sambo, but not being able to account for them at the time he kept to the original trail. The next day showed the party the circle made by the boys, and then they followed on until Sambo came to the place where they had met with the two wild black men. He exhibited his uneasiness so plainly that Mr. Everdale asked him what was the matter.

"Poor feller boys, those!" he said. "No good look about any more for um; no see um again. Wild black fellers been along here; boys knock long a-head now—no good go further."

Sambo pointed out tracks of naked feet, then they found the ashes of the fire, and Sambo pointed to where the natives and the boys had sat around it. The trail leading away and showing the marks of the boys' boots and the naked feet of the blacks was tolerably plain to Smith, and upon a piece of sandy ground Mr. Everdale could see for himself that Sambo was speaking the truth.

A council of war was now held as to what was best to be done. Sambo flatly refused to follow the trail a step further. He said that the wild blacks would kill the whole party as soon as they were met with; they were very fierce and very strong, and he, Sambo, was not going to endanger his life. Not all Mr. Everdale's offers of tobacco, nor Smith's threats of vengeance, could shake his resolution—go he would not. It was no use forcing him; he simply would not track, and very possibly would lead the searchers astray. Mr. Everdale was for leaving him at once and following the trail with Smith as best he could.

But here the stockman pointed out that that plan would hardly do. It would be madness for two unarmed men to go in amongst wild blacks in a strange country. The best thing to do would be to hurry back to Willaroo, get their revolvers and rifles, some more men, and additional food. This loss of time appeared terrible to Mr. Everdale, but after a little reflection he saw that it would be the best plan in the end, and adopted it. They, of course, knew whereabouts they

were, and by riding straight across country greatly lessened the distance to Willaroo. On his arrival Mr Everdale found that two of his friends from adjoining stations had come over to assist in the search, and at once volunteered to go back with him on the following day. Indeed, every man on the station wanted to go, not only because the boys were related to the master, and also that they were general favourites, but because all bushmen are ready to do everything to recover a missing man.

Cowardly Sambo was left at Willaroo, and besides Mr. Everdale the party contained his two friends, Smith, and one other man. They took two spare horses with them to carry the rugs and provisions, and to mount the boys upon when found. The point from where Mr. Everdale and Smith had turned back was reached on the following day, and then began the work of tracking.

It is not necessary that we should follow them throughout their long journey. They travelled at a slower pace than the boys had done with the natives, but they tried to balance this by rising before dawn to eat their breakfast, and taking up the trail as soon as the light was strong enough. A few minutes' rest for dinner at noon would be taken, and then on again till sunset.

They now came upon the tracks of the natives who

had set out on their expedition for red ochre. These they followed, hoping to find the boys with them, or at least gain news concerning them. They overtook the men at the end of a long day's ride, and at first it appeared as if a fight would take place. The natives drew themselves up in battle array. The white men unslung their carbines and loaded them. Happily, however, one of Mr. Everdale's friends knew a little of the language, sufficient to make the natives understand the object of their search, and to assure them they did not intend to do them harm.

Great was the joy of the searchers on hearing that when the men had left the camp the white boys were alive and well. Then they parted with the blacks with expressions of goodwill, and turned in the direction of the camp. They arrived there on the morning following the night on which Ralph and Ernest had made their escape. As soon as they caught sight of the smoke from the fires they galloped down, in order to prevent the blacks running away into the scrub and perhaps taking their prisoners with them. To a looker-on the scene at the camp would have been most ludicrous. Catching up their weapons, children, and anything else that was easily carried, the natives scuttled off in all directions. Mr. Everdale and one man rode straight to the wurleys to look for the boys, and Smith chased one of the old men. The old man ran well, dropping his spears and waddies as he went so as to lighten himself. But the horseman was too swift for him, and, being completely out of breath, the native tumbled heels over head into a bush.

Smith picked him up, patted him on the back, and laughed and spoke to him in English to assure him that he need not fear. But the old man was terribly afraid, and shivered and shook from head to foot.

Mr. Everdale meanwhile had not found the boys. The native was questioned, but it was some time before he could be induced to speak. When he did they understood him to say that the boys had escaped during the night.

This was tolerably good news if it was true, and the only way to prove it was to make this native track the runaways. They explained this, and the old man seemed not to have any objection now that he was assured the strangers had no intention of doing him an injury The other natives could be seen looking on from behind bushes and trees, expecting probably to see their friend killed at any moment But now the man called one of the others to him, and after exchanging some words they began to track . . . . hind the other, and if the leader lost the trail the other seemed to recover it at once, and then assumed the foremost place. The boys were not to be seen as the evening closed in. The natives were fastened each by one leg to a tree, and the whites took it in turns to mount guard over them through the night.

CHAPTER XXIII.

THE MIRAGE.

WE left the boys just as they had got safely past the firelight into the darkness; but they continued to crawl for some distance, because in that way they could proceed with less noise than on foot. At last they considered themselves safe and rose from the ground.

"We are saved! We are saved!" Ernest said, in a whisper.

"Don't holloa before you are out of the wood." Ralph replied. "If an alarm was given those blacks would catch us up in no time."

"Don't you think we ought to thank God for having preserved us, and helped us to get away?"

"I have already done so, Ern; it would be madness to stop and kneel down, we must pray as we go. There is no irreverence in it, for God can read our hearts."

"I don't know at all. We must go on till daylight, and then try to fix our course."

All through the night they travelled, walking quickly, and where the ground was not too stony they would run for a short distance. The grey dawn saw them toiling through a tangled scrub, and the blazing sun at noon saw them, faint and weary, crossing a sandy plain. They had stopped merely for a few minutes now and then. Repeatedly as the day went on did they look back to see if the natives were on their track, but nothing could they see. The vast melancholy bush lay all around them, and it was difficult to suppose that human beings were living and moving not so very far away from them. Twice they had chanced to find water, but it was almost undrinkable, being thick with mud, and a green scum resting on the surface. These small holes would be dry in a day or two, and the boys wondered vaguely as to the trials that lay before them. Their sojourn with the blacks enabled them to find food, but they confined themselves to roots and berries, because even if they had had the means they dare not light a fire to cook rats or lizards.

On the second night Nature insisted upon being obeyed, and our boys slept for an hour or two, but no longer. Ralph awoke from a dream in which he had played in a cricket match, and soon had been clean-bowled. He aroused Ernest, and then they trudged on again.

But their pace was slower than on the previous day. The roots barely satisfied their hunger, and did not afford sufficient nourishment to support them under such trying circumstances. Worse than all, however, was the feeling of thirst. The last water they had found was at noon on the day previous, and since then they had had none.

Neither of the boys spoke a word more than was absolutely necessary—indeed, they could hardly speak at all. Ralph always took the lead, and Ernest followed; to-day he lagged terribly behind, his head ached, his eyes seemed to be balls of fire, stones and sticks wounded his feet through the holes in his worn-out boots; strange fancies began to flit through his mind.

Ralph, too, was feeling that he could not go much farther, but he was stronger than his cousin. Leaning against a tree he waited for Ernest to come up to him. Seeing a look of gladness in the boy's eyes, Ralph said, in a husky voice, "What is it, Ern?"

"Don't you hear it, Ralph? There! the station bell! It must be dinner-time, I think. We've walked a long way, haven't we? I wonder what aunt will say when we get back?"

"There is no bell ringing, Ern; it is only fancy. We are a long way from the station yet. I wish—oh, how I wish we could find some water!"

"Well, let's go down to the lake and get some."

"What lake?"

"There—don't you see it?"

Ralph turned, and saw, not a mile away, a beautiful blue sheet of water! The deception was perfect; it looked like a lake nestling at the foot of a low hill. The trees surrounding it were reflected in its depths. Ernest was already moving towards it. Ralph laid his hand upon his cousin's arm.

"Don't go: it is only a mirage. It is out of our way, too!"

"Don't tell me! It is water! I shall go I'm dying for a drink—my throat's on fire. Leave go!"

Ernest pulled away his arm from Ralph's grasp as he spoke, and again went towards the mirage. How beautiful it looked to him! how delicious would it be to drink again and again of its clear water, and to bathe in it! Full of these thoughts, and his longing growing more intense as he gazed, Ernest tried to run, that he might more quickly reach the shore. But he had hardly gone a few yards before he became dizzy; everything raced round before him in confusion; he made one

desperate attempt to keep up, and then fell fainting to the ground.

Ralph was beside him at once, startled and horrified, as the thought rushed through his mind that Ernest was dead. Exhausted as he was, he managed to half lift, half drag the unconscious boy to the shade of a tree. There he seated himself, and rested Ernest's head upon his knee. What else could he do? Nothing! There was no water to put to his lips, no clothes to be loosed; he must wait until he came round again, if ever he did so.

Ernest opened his eyes after a while. "Are we at the station, Ralph?" he asked feebly.

Ernest sighed wearily, and asked no more questions By-and-by he tried to rise with Ralph's assistance, but he was unable to walk, his legs refused to obey his will, and with a moan he again sank down. Ralph placed his arm around him, and leaning back against a tree supported Ernest for a time. He felt that their fate was sealed, but the feeling did not disturb him All he experienced was the craving for water; no thoughts of home, no faces of friends flitted before his mind's eye; they were nothing compared to a cup of water.

The boys were in that position when the sun went down; when it rose again they were stretched out side by side, their arms thrown round each other. The light fell upon their faces, but they did not awake; little lizards peeped from beneath the bark of the tree, and with increasing confidence came forth and crawled upon the motionless boys; the great iguanas, of which the boys had often eaten lately, crawled along the ground, and with their snake-like heads raised, and cloven tongues darting in and out of their mouths, gazed at them with black, beady, expressionless eyes. Suddenly two black crows flew past, swooping down close to the boys, and then with a hoarse cry perched upon a tree close by; other crows followed in quick succession, until the trees were laden with them.

CHAPTER XXIV.

FOUND

FAR overhead, in the fathomless blue, four eagles described great circles as they glanced at what was passing upon the earth beneath them. They saw the motionless bodies, the lizards, and the crows, but besides those they saw two black men and a party of horsemen slowly crossing the plain in the direction of where the boys lay. Soon they emerge from a belt of scrub, and a crow, high perched, catches sight of them; it utters a note of warning, and the whole assembly rise into the air like a black cloud.

"Look! Look!" exclaimed Smith to Mr Everdale. "D'ye see them crows? The boys are there!"

"Not dead! not dead, I pray, O God!" was all the answer that Mr. Everdale could make, half to himself, as spurring his horse he galloped forward with Smith closely following. They came to the tree beneath which lay the boys; the lizards and iguanas scuttled away, the men threw themselves from their horses, and as Mr. Everdale knelt down to feel if his son's heart still beat, Smith unstrapped the water-bag from his saddle.

"They are yet alive!" exclaimed Mr. Everdale in a tone of thankfulness. "Quick, Smith! the water!"

As he spoke, he drenched his neck-handkerchief with water, and then squeezed a few drops into the parched mouths of the unconscious boys. The rest of the searchers had come up by this time, and formed an interesting group. The whites were gathered round doing all that was possible to revive the lads; the blacks, leaning on their spears, looked on with faces that betokened no expression of surprise or sympathy; the horses cropped the bushes and shrubs, making good use of their spare time; the crows "cawed" their discontent; and the eagles, taking wider circles, searched for other food.

Ralph was the first to open his eyes, and used them to stare at the faces around him in blank amazement. "I'm dreaming!" they heard him murmur.

"Not a bit of it, my boy!" said Mr. Everdale. "Rouse up, and we'll soon be homeward bound!"

The two last words seemed to have a magical effect. Ralph sat up, and Ernest opened his eyes at last. And how they craved for one long drink from the bags!

But this was not permitted. Mr. Everdale at first would only give them little sips, and to the boys this seemed the refinement of cruelty. By evening they were able to eat a little food, and after that soon gained strength.

The services of the trackers were no longer necessary, and they were dismissed after being made happy by a present of a tomahawk and sheath knife. The party stayed where they were that night, and then at daybreak set their faces homeward.

"Are we far from Willaroo, father?" asked Ralph.

"About one hundred and fifty miles," Mr. Everdale replied; "and we should have been still further away if you two lads had kept on walking. Smart bushmen you'll make if you don't learn to find your way across country better than you have done."

"Were we going in the wrong direction, then?"

"Yes, you were walking away from home as fast as you could go. And now I should like to know what induced you to leave the track to hunt a kangaroo in the scrub?"

"Why, father! it was that white kangaroo, you know!"

"Well, blest if I didn't think so!" exclaimed Smith. "It's time that 'ere animal was shot. There's been that amount of talk about it, and it's escaped so often, that folks really begin to think it's got a charmed life."

It was a four-days' journey to Willaroo, and the boys were quite themselves again by the time they reached it. At the camp fires of an evening they told of their experiences amongst the blacks, and had an attentive and interested audience.

"Well," said Mr. Everdale, at the conclusion of the story, "they are a curious race of people. And I do not see what can be done for them, except that we must treat them kindly, and not render their life more miserable than it is. They have no religion, and therefore no hope. They know not of a past, nor do they think of a future."

CHAPTER XXV.

THE WHITE KANGAROO.

THERE is no more to tell, except to say that, as the party passed through the Never Never Ranges, the white kangaroo paid them a visit. It was at night; every man was asleep, except Smith, who had risen to throw a fresh log on the fire. As he was making himself comfortable again in his rugs he heard something hopping about, and looking in the direction saw the ghostly visitor sitting erect within the light of the fire.

He reached for his carbine, lying beneath his saddle at his head, took careful aim, and fired. The kangaroo made one convulsive bound and fell dead, shot through the heart. But the effect of this sudden shot upon the sleepers was tremendous. They thought of nothing less than a charge of wild blacks, and as they sprang up they grasped their carbines, and stared out into the darkness.

"Who fired?" asked Mr. Everdale.

"I did," answered Smith.

"What for, in the name of wonder?"

"Had a bit of a dream, sir. What those young gents told us about Kootchie must have scared me, I fancy. Anyway, I thought I saw a ghost standing yonder, just by that twisted mallee. I was a bit scared at first, then I said I'd let drive just to see if it were a ghost. Perhaps you wouldn't mind looking, Mr. Ralph, just to see if I hit anything."

The kangaroo was soon found and dragged into the light. It was pure white from its head to the tip of the tail, and its eyes were pink.

"I shall skin this fellow now," said Ralph, "just to show that it hadn't a charmed life, and also as a memento of the day we were lost in the bush."

On the following day they arrived at the station. The dogs were the first to welcome them, rushing out in a pack, and showing their joy in mad gambols and incessant barking. As they passed the kitchen the men came out and cheered them, and shook the lads by the hand till their arms were almost out of joint. The maid-servants could be seen looking for them from the back of the house, and Ralph was certain that he could see his mother standing in the drawing-room, back from the window. The boys, at a hint from Mr. Everdale, let their horses go, and ran to the house, and, I need hardly say, met with a reception that very much tried their manliness.

Mr. Everdale and his friends stayed away at the stables for twenty minutes or so, to give Mrs. Everdale and her boys time to recover.

Three days after their return the first day of a New Year dawned upon Willaroo. The squatters from many neighbouring stations came at the invitation of Mr. Everdale, and helped to mark the New Year and the safe return of the boys with a pleasant festival; and Ralph and Ernest, for about the twentieth time, related how they were lost and kept by the blacks, and all owing to the pursuit of the White Kangaroo.

THE END.

WELLS GARDNER, DARTON & CO.'S

LIST OF ATTRACTIVE

REWARD BOOKS.

3s. 6d. PRIZE BOOKS.

IN SPLENDID BINDINGS.

THE "HONOR BRIGHT" SERIES.

Large crown 8vo, cloth boards, 3s. 6d.

Gilly Flower.

By the Author of "Honor Bright," &c. Illustrated Title and Frontispiece by GORDON BROWNE.

"'Gilly Flower' is quite up to the standard of the author's previous works."—STANDARD.

Large crown 8vo, extra cloth boards, 3s. 6d.

One of a Covey.

By the Author of "Honor Bright," "Peas-Blossom," &c. With Thirty Original Illustrations by H. J. A. MILES.

"Full of spirit and life, so well sustained throughout that grown-up readers may enjoy it as much as children. It is one of the best books of the season."—GUARDIAN.

"We have rarely read a story for boys and girls with greater pleasure. One of the chief characters would not have disgraced Dickens' pen."
—LITERARY WORLD.

Wells Gardner, Darton & Co.'s Publications.

Large crown 8vo, cloth boards, 3s. 6d.

Honor Bright; or, the Four-leaved Shamrock.

By the Author of "One of a Covey," "Robin and Linnet," &c. With Illustrated Title Page and Frontispiece.
[Sixth Edition.

"A cheery, sensible, and healthy tale."—THE TIMES.

Large crown 8vo, cloth boards, 3s. 6d.

N. or M.

By the Author of "Honor Bright," "Peas-Blossom," "One of a Covey," &c. With Thirty Original Illustrations by H. J. A. MILES.

"A most thoroughly charming and delightful tale . . . Nolly and Molly are two bright, happy girls, full of fun and merriment, and not too good to be altogether acceptable to youthful readers . . . The illustrations are plentiful, and are of a quality that will prove entirely satisfactory to young readers. . . . In every way an acceptable gift book."—GUARDIAN.

Large crown 8vo, cloth boards, 3s. 6d.

Peas-Blossom.

By the Author of "Honor Bright," "One of a Covey," &c. With Thirty Original Illustrations by H. J. A. MILES.

"'Peas-blossom' may be described as a rollickingly respectable Irish story, the names of the juvenile pair of heroes being Pat and Paddy Like the young Anthony Trollope, they are sent to a school five miles away from their homes across country, and are even more regardless than he of personal appearance. On one occasion they swim a river, when a bridge has been washed away, and walk onwards in their wet clothes . . and so we are carried on to the end through an exceptionally readable volume"
—THE TIMES.

Paternoster Buildings.

Wells Gardner, Darton & Co.'s Publications.

Large crown 8vo, cloth boards, 3s. 6d.

Dogged Jack.

By FRANCES PALMER. Illustrated.　　[Second Edition.

"There is no boy who could fail to be interested in 'Dogged Jack.'"
—CHRISTIAN WORLD.

Large crown 8vo, cloth boards, 3s. 6d.

True Under Trial.

By FRANCES PALMER. Illustrated.　　[Fifth Edition.

"A well written story."—THE TIMES.

"One of the best boy's books we have seen for a long time. The adventures of little Edward Forbes, who was 'true under trial,' are written with such knowledge of the details of London life among the destitute orders; with such rare combination of religious spirit, with a perfect abstention from cant, and so well put together, that we believe no reader who once took up the book would put it down without finishing it."—STANDARD.

Large crown 8vo, cloth boards, 3s. 6d.

Count up the Sunny Days.

A Story for Boys and Girls. By C. A. JONES. With Illustrated Title Page and Frontispiece.　　[Second Edition.

"A capital story for boys and girls. It is interesting from beginning to end."—SCOTSMAN.

"Thoroughly deserving of commendation."—SPECTATOR.

Large crown 8vo, cloth boards, 3s. 6d.

Little Jeanneton's Work.

A Chronicle of Breton Life. By C. A. JONES. With upwards of Thirty Illustrations.

"This 'Chronicle of Breton Life' is a story of the old régime. Jeanneton is a farmer's daughter, and being taken up by the great people at

Wells Gardner, Darton & Co.'s Publications.

Large crown 8vo, cloth boards, 3s. 6d.

The Old Ship; or, Better than Strength.

By H. A. FORDE. With Eight full-page Tinted Illustrations.

"The incidents and descriptions of schoolboy life are really good."
—RECORD

"A handsome volume."—CHURCH TIMES.

Large crown 8vo, extra cloth boards, 3s. 6d.

Edith Vernon's Life Work.

By the Author of "Harry's Battles," "Susie's Flowers," &c., &c. Illustrated. [Twelfth Edition.

"A very pretty story, very well told."—LITERARY CHURCHMAN.

Large crown 8vo, cloth boards extra, 3s. 6d.

A Lost Piece of Silver.

By the Author of "Edith Vernon's Life Work," &c. Illustrated.

"Told without exaggeration, without any fine writing, but with considerable power."—SPECTATOR.

Large crown 8vo, cloth boards, 3s. 6d.

Only a Girl.

A Story of a Quiet Life. A Tale of Brittany. Adapted from the French by C. A. JONES. With upwards of Forty Illustrations.

"We can thoroughly recommend this brightly-written and homely narrative."—SATURDAY REVIEW.

Paternoster Buildings.

Wells Gardner, Darton & Co.'s Publications.

NEW EDITIONS OF JEAN INGELOW'S BOOKS FOR GIRLS.

Large crown 8vo, cloth boards, 3s. 6d

Studies for Stories.

From Girls' Lives. By JEAN INGELOW. Illustrated Title and Frontispiece from drawings by GORDON BROWNE.

Large crown 8vo, cloth boards, 3s 6d.

A Sister's Bye-hours.

By JEAN INGELOW. Illustrated Title and Frontispiece from drawings by GORDON BROWNE.

Large crown 8vo, cloth boards, 3s. 6d.

Sue and I.

By Mrs. O'REILLY Illustrated Title and Frontispiece.

"A thoroughly delightful book, full of sound wisdom as well as fun"
—ATHENÆUM

Large crown 8vo, extra cloth boards, gilt edges, 3s. 6d.

Out of the Way.

A Village Story. By H L TAYLOR. With Twenty-four Original Illustrations by A. H. COLLINS.

"Really an interesting story. . . . Excellently carried out . We were half way through the book before we found out that it was a temperance tale at all"—GUARDIAN.

"The book deserves warm praise; we wish there were more temperance tales like it."—CHRISTIAN WORLD.

Paternoster Buildings.

Wells Gardner, Darton & Co.'s Publications.

JAMES F. COBB'S BOOKS OF ADVENTURE.

In Most Attractive Bindings.

Large crown 8vo, cloth boards, 3s. 6d.

Martin the Skipper.

A Tale for Boys and Seafaring Folk. Five full-page Illustrations by G. L. SEYMOUR and A. H. COLLINS.

[Sixth Edition.

"We should imagine those queer folk indeed who could not read this story with eager interest and pleasure, be they boys or girls, young or old. We highly commend the style in which the book is written, and the religious spirit which pervades it."—CHRISTIAN WORLD

Large crown 8vo, cloth boards, 3s. 6d.

Off to California.

A Tale of the Gold Country. Adapted from the Flemish of Hendrik Conscience. Illustrated with Six full-page Plates by A. FORESTIER.

"The scene of this story is laid in exciting times. The adventurers go through the greatest perils; and find a wonderful treasure in the pool of a mountain . . This is a good story of its kind, told with spirit, and admirable in tone and moral."—SPECTATOR

"This is a capital story for boys, full of adventure and stirring incident, but of excellent tone and good moral tendency. There are half-a-dozen spirited illustrations, and the book is attractively bound."—NONCONFORMIST.

Large crown 8vo, cloth, bevelled boards, 3s. 6d.

The Watchers on the Longships.

A Tale of Cornwall in the last Century. Illustrated with Four full-page Engravings by DAVIDSON KNOWLES.

[Fifteenth Edition.

"A capital story, and one we heartily commend to boy readers, both gentle and simple."—GUARDIAN.

Paternoster Buildings.

CPSIA information can be obtained at www.ICGtesting.com
Printed in the USA
LVOW02s2117201113

362115LV00018B/908/P